CREATING YOUR
FUTURE

GEORGE L. MORRISEY, CSP, CPAE

CREATING YOUR
FUTURE

Personal Strategic Planning
for Professionals

George L. Morrisey

Berrett-Koehler Publishers
San Francisco

Berrett-Koehler Publishers, Inc.
155 Montgomery St.
San Francisco, CA 94104-4109

Ordering Information
Orders by individuals and organizations. Berrett-Koehler publications are available through bookstores or can be ordered direct from the publisher at the Berrett-Koehler address or by calling 1 (800) 929-2929.

Quantity sales. Berrett-Koehler publications are available at special quantity discounts when purchased in bulk by corporations, associations, and others. For details, write to the "Special Sales Department" at the Berrett-Koehler address above or call (415) 288-0260.

Orders by U.S. trade bookstores and wholesalers. Please contact Prima WorldWide, P.O. Box 1260, Rocklin, CA 95677-1260; tel. (916) 786-0426; fax (916) 786-0488.

Orders for college textbook/course adoption use. Please contact Berrett-Koehler Publishers, 155 Montgomery St., San Francisco, CA 94104-4109; tel (415) 288-0260; fax (415) 362-2512.

Printed in the United States of America

Printed on acid-free and recycled paper that meets the strictest state and U.S. guidelines for recycled paper (50 percent recycled waste, including 10 percent post-consumer waste).

Library of Congress Cataloging-in-Publication Data

Morrisey, George L.
    Creating your future : personal strategic planning for
professionals / George L. Morrisey : foreword by Edward E. Scannell.
        p. cm.
    Includes bibliographical references and index.
    ISBN 1–881052–06–0 (alk. paper)
    1. Strategic planning. 2. Career development. I. Title.
    HD30.28.M648   1992
    650.1—dc20   92–19057
                                                    CIP

First Edition
First Printing 1992

Illustrations copyright © 1992 by Jim Carpenter
Photograph copyright © 1992 by Paul Buddle
Book design and production by Pacific West Publishing Service, Eugene, Oregon

This book is dedicated to the memory of
Dr. George S. Odiorne
my colleague, my mentor, my friend

Contents

1. Introduction–
The Case for Personal Strategic Planning   1

- Why me?
- What are some of the benefits of or considerations in personal strategic planning?
- What are some concerns we, as professionals, have with personal strategic planning?
- Who else needs to be involved?
- How about a strategic planning notebook?
- In summary

2. Determining Your Professional Direction   11

- What are your professional career options?
  - For the professional employee within a diversified organization
  - For the independent, self-employed professional
  - For the professional within a professional services firm
- Exercise – Getting your directional focus
- In summary

3. Assessing Your Strategic Values   27

- What guides your professional decision-making now?
- What should guide your decision-making?
- How do you prioritize your own strategic values?
- What do you need to do to change your strategic direction?

Foreword

FOR MANY OF US, the term "Strategic Planning" conjures up images of those intense sessions in which important managers from across the globe chart the future directions of their respective corporate giants. That these same principles and tools could have an equally important application to us as individuals is a thought most of us seldom consider.

It seems fitting, then, that George Morrisey, whose name is all but synonymous with "Strategic Planning," should take these same ingredients and offer them as practical tools for use in our own individual careers. With fourteen books already to his credit, this newest offering is one you don't just read – you digest! His highly readable style, coupled with his proven and pragmatic usable content, always sets his books apart. This book is no exception to that mode. You have in your hands that power and information to strategically create and manage your own future.

As you read through these pages, you'll quickly come to know George Morrisey as do hundreds of his faithful followers. You will see him up close, both personally and professionally. Drawing on his vast experience in both the private and public sectors, George gives his readers a highly usable blueprint for action. His consulting assignments have taken him around the world, but his sage counsel and advice are very much "down home".

Through his activities and involvement with a number of professional organizations, notably the American Society for Training and Development and the National Speakers Association, he has been a colleague, guru, mentor, and most important, a friend to all of us. As you begin "Creating Your Future" (and have fun doing it), you're in for a solid treat; and you'll make a new friend in the process.

Edward E. Scannell, C.M.P. (Certified Meeting Professional), C.S.P. (Certified Speaking Professional), Past President of the American Society for Training and Development, Meeting Planners International, and the National Speakers Association.

Preface

STRATEGIC PLANNING is a common practice in business. While it may not always be practiced effectively, it is generally acknowledged that taking a long term look at where the organization should be headed is an essential consideration for any viable enterprise. If we accept this principle as being appropriate in business, why is it that most of us do not appear to accept this same principle as being equally applicable in that most important business of all – the pursuit of our own careers and personal lives?

Actually, we do look ahead, of course. At various times in our lives, we all develop dreams of what we would like to become, particularly as it applies to our careers. After all, that is one of the prime motivators we have in making choices related to education, specialized training, job experience and professional affiliations. However, we seldom go through the discipline required to make things happen. Dreaming is an important part of the strategic planning process, but planning must go well beyond the dream to translate it into reality. "Wishing will make it so" only happens in the movies. But, unfortunately, wishing is where the process stops for many individuals.

This book is specifically designed to help you develop a future-oriented perspective related to all aspects of your life including, but not limited to, your career. It will address such questions as:

- What are my career options?
- How do I prepare myself for my next career step?
- What do I need to know and do about my personal and business finances?
- Where does my family fit in?
- How can I keep my career, business and personal life in proper balance?

- How can I improve my professional credibility so I am worth more in the marketplace?
- Is private practice the right course for me?
- Should I consider joining a professional services firm?
- What if I decide to stay where I am? What do I do next?

In looking at questions such as these, please recognize that this book will not give you precise answers to any of them. My perspective, as a management consultant, is that it is far more important for me to make certain you are asking yourself the right questions than to provide you with the right answers. In planning, the process is far more important than the product. There is a familiar analogy that appears in the writings of most religions – "I can give you a fish and feed you for a day or I can teach you how to fish and feed you for a lifetime." My desire is to make you a "fisherman or woman" as you proceed through this book.

For Whom Is This Book Written and How Can It Be Used?

While, theoretically, the concepts and techniques covered in this book can be used by anyone at any stage in their life, its greatest appeal will be to professionals and entrepreneurs, with at least some college education, who have been in the world of work for a period of time. These may include professionals such as accountants, attorneys, engineers, health care professionals, sales people, systems analysts, administrators and managers, educators, trainers, planners or a variety of others. If any of the following situations, or others like them, are typical of where you are or might soon be in your career, you will find this book useful in moving you to the next step. If you:

- are in your first full-time professional position;
- are trying to determine whether or not you should go into management with your current employer or with another;
- are at a midpoint in your career and no longer feel challenged in your current job;
- have an opportunity to make an attractive job change

and want to evaluate your options;

- have already decided to make a job or career change;
- may be faced with the possibility of voluntary or involuntary job loss;
- want to be in the professional services business;
- are thinking of entering private practice;
- want to further develop your existing practice;
- want to achieve a more meaningful balance between your career, your business and your personal life;
- are approaching normal retirement age and want to plan specifically what you will do with the rest of your life.

I will focus on three primary career models:

- a professional, such as an administrator or trainer, employed within a diversified organization;
- a professional, such as an accountant, who is now in, or is considering going into, private practice;
- a professional, such as an attorney, who is now, or is considering becoming, a part of a professional services firm.

Overview of the Contents

The chapters in this book are designed to lead you through the personal strategic planning process in a logical and sequential order. However, for most people it is neither practical nor desirable to attempt to produce a complete strategic plan as a first effort. You will probably find it much more meaningful to approach the development of your plan in a series of bite-sized pieces, concentrating initially on those steps that will get you moving in the right direction. The chapters are structured so you can use them selectively in constructing a plan that is uniquely and powerfully yours.

Chapter 1 is a good starting place, of course. I recommend that you read it first. It provides an overview of the process we will be following as well as some of the benefits and concerns associated with it. It also suggests the importance of getting others involved and of setting up a strategic planning notebook to keep your plans organized in a useful way.

Chapter 2 explores the various career options that may be available to you, including some you may not have considered previously. You will also find a valuable checklist entitled "Your Career Path Options" which will help you identify where you are now in your career and establish a focus for your future career direction.

Chapter 3 will help you identify the personal values that could or should influence your thinking as you begin to create your future. Then, through an interesting forced-choice decision-making process, you will be able to determine the relative importance of each, leading eventually to the determination of your personal "driving force", that one value which will be the ultimate determinant of your future career direction.

Chapter 4 shows you how to prepare your personal and professional mission statement. In my judgment, a mission statement is the single most important document in a strategic plan, whether for a business or an individual. It provides you with a foundation for making sound decisions on where you want to go with your career and your life.

Chapter 5 will help you set some initial priorities on areas of strategic concern within four major headings: Personal, Career Growth, Business Development, and Financial. You will need to isolate those particular areas that are of vital importance to you personally before you focus on specific long term objectives and actions that may be appropriate for you.

Chapters 6 through 9 go into considerably more detail related to critical issues you may be facing in each of the above-referenced four major headings. Included are several examples of issue analysis from a wide variety of professionals as well as some specific analytical tools which you can use. You will probably want to deal with the material in these four chapters on a highly selective basis.

Chapter 10 shows you how to develop long term objectives which will position you wherever you want to be at some point in the future related to the critical issues you have identified.

Chapter 11 focuses on what you must do to reach your long term objectives. From these strategic action plans, you can build some bridges to what you need to accomplish in both the short and long term.

Chapter 12 ties your whole plan together and provides guidelines on when and how to modify your plans.

The Appendix includes reproducible copies of all the worksheets covered in the book as well as an Annotated Bibliography of other resources you may wish to make use of.

Why Was This Book Written?

Many, if not most, self-help books have been written, I am sure, to satisfy a current, prior or future personal need of the author. I have spent approximately half of my professional life as a specialist or a manager within diversified organizations and the remaining half as a consultant/speaker/trainer in private practice. My experience with professional services firms has been through personal contact with several such organizations plus an abortive attempt to build one myself (I will share some of my experience in that arena later on). While I am very happy and fulfilled where I am now in my career, it was not always so. A certain amount of pain and frustration is inevitable and even desirable during career growth. However, a book like this might have kept me from stumbling quite so often.

Also, in recent years I have become more acutely aware of the importance of achieving and maintaining a balanced life, an awareness I did not have during my earlier years when I tended to practice career tunnel vision. Fortunately, I have been blessed with a sensitive and supportive wife who has helped me work through the tough periods and is now my partner in a mutually-fulfilling life style. Furthermore, as I approach my more mature years, some of the concepts and techniques covered in this book were developed to help me make the kinds of modifications in both my personal and professional life that will make that life a continuous exciting adventure.

This book has been three years (plus a lifetime) in the making. It is very meaningful to me. I hope it will be meaningful to you as well.

George L. Morrisey
Buena Park, California
June 1992

Acknowledgments

MY THANKS to the thousands of professionals who have participated in my seminar and consulting efforts over the years who have given me a rich legacy of experience to share with you here. I am particularly grateful to:

- the members of my professional support group – Tom Callister, Jane Holcomb, Eileen McDargh, Jack Mixner and Karen Wilson – who have provided continued encouragement as well as very constructive feedback during the development of this book;

- my long time friend and colleague, Ed Scannell, for helping me stretch professionally and for his much-appreciated Foreword;

- my many other friends and colleagues in the National Speakers Association and elsewhere who have provided me with specific feedback during the evolution of this book resulting in a much stronger and more practical approach;

- and, finally and most importantly, my wife, Carol, my best friend, my severest critic, and the one who makes my present and my future really worth living.

The Author

GEORGE L. MORRISEY, CSP, CPAE, is a management consultant, professional speaker and seminar leader who specializes in the areas of strategic and operational planning for organizations and individuals. He is Chairman of The Morrisey Group, a management consulting firm based in Southern California. His background includes more than 20 years as a practicing manager and key specialist with several organizations in both the private and public sectors in addition to more than 20 years as a full time consultant. He has personally assisted more than 200 business, industrial, service, governmental and not-for-profit organizations in planning process implementation.

Morrisey is the author, or co-author, of fourteen prior books, including The Executive Guide to Strategic Planning, The Executive Guide to Operational Planning, Management by Objectives and Results for Business and Industry, Management by Objectives and Results in the Public Sector, Performance Appraisals for Business and Industry, Performance Appraisals in the Public Sector, Effective Business and Technical Presentations, and Getting Your Act Together: Goal Setting for Fun, Health and Profit (which complements the popular Salenger Educational Media film with the same title, which features Morrisey and for which he served as adviser). He is the author and producer of several audio and videocassette learning programs, all directed toward helping individuals and organizations become more effective and self-fulfilled.

Morrisey was granted B.S. (1951) and M.Ed. (1952) degrees from Springfield College in Massachusetts. A professional's professional, he received the Certified Speaking Professional (CSP) designation in 1983 and was recognized in 1984 with the Council of Peers Award for Excellence (CPAE), the highest recognition granted to a professional speaker by the National Speakers Association. He was also the recipient of the national

American Society for Training Development (ASTD) Award for Publications in 1974. He has served as a member of the Boards of Directors of the Association for Management Excellence (formerly the International MBO Institute) and the National Speakers Association.

If you would like to know more about George Morrisey and his speaking and consulting services, please contact him at The Morrisey Group, P. O. Box 5879, Buena Park, CA 90622-5879, (800) 535-8202 or (in California) (714) 995-1244.

CHAPTER 1

Introduction

The Case
for Personal
Strategic
Planning

Why Me?

- You've got to be kidding!
- Strategic planning – that's for big corporations, isn't it? What's that got to do with me? I'm just a small fish in a big pond! What influence can I have?
- Survival is the name of the game for me! This year I'll worry about this year; next year I'll worry about next year; the year after that doesn't exist!

THOUGHTS SUCH AS THESE may very well cross your mind when the subject of long term strategic planning for you personally is raised. Whether you are an independent professional in a one-person operation, a partner or staff member in a professional services firm, or a professional operating within a large or small corporation or governmental agency, you may wonder why you should put any effort into it. What's the payoff for you? How can this help you achieve things that otherwise might have slipped by?

My plan in this book is to share with you the benefits of applying the principles of strategic planning to yourself personally and to provide a methodology which can work for *you*, with significant benefits both now and in the future. (You may find it useful to develop your own planning notebook – looseleaf recommended – so you can record your ideas as you proceed.)

"Strategic planning" is a concept that most professionals are familiar with, although its personal application may not have been obvious. Its effectiveness depends on systematic thinking, a discipline that is common to most professions. Its purpose, in business, is to examine the future and develop plans that will help make that future as productive, fulfilling and profitable as possible. Since the most important business you will ever manage is your own life, it is only logical, as Mr. Spock would say, to take that concept and make it work for you, personally, in *Creating Your Future*.

As we begin, let me offer one caveat. Never *adopt* any planning system. Rather, *adapt* whatever system is proposed in a way that makes sense for you. Your knowledge, experience, personal style, temperament, and the circumstances in which you find yourself will all shape the way your personal planning system should be designed. Always keep in mind that plans are a means to an end, never an end in themselves. If you can keep your focus on where plans are leading, without getting hung up on the mechanics of the process, you'll find that this approach will open up huge new vistas in terms of both present and future satisfaction in your life.

What Are Some of the Benefits of or Considerations in Personal Strategic Planning?

First of all, strategic planning helps provide a **personal vision** for the future. It is so easy to get wrapped up in the present that we lose sight of where the future might be leading. If we intend to grow in any significant aspect of our lives, we need to focus periodically on what the future will look like. Depending on where you are in your career and your life, this future vision may be as little as two or three years out or as much as twenty or thirty years in the future. The ironic thing about focusing on a period in the future is that what you project for that time is probably not what's going to happen. Specific

circumstances, opportunities, setbacks, and personal preferences may lead you in a distinctly different direction from that
established in your initial plan. That does not invalidate the
planning process. By focusing on the future, we are able to
determine when it is appropriate to change course. *Change and
modification are an essential ingredient of any effective planning
process.*

Career direction is a strong concern for most professionals, particularly during the early stages of their careers. It is
interesting to note that only a small fraction of professionals
end up in the career for which they initially prepared. Our
interests change; different opportunities present themselves;
family obligations impact the direction in which we are moving. By looking forward, we have a better chance of identifying
some of the road blocks that may keep us from realizing our
original goals while, at the same time, create new opportunities. Sometimes, by playing the "what if" game, new vistas will
open up that might not otherwise have been apparent. While
this will not necessarily prevent us from stumbling along the
way, it will increase the likelihood that we will be able to
respond more effectively to things that can significantly impact
where we are going.

For example, I have made two major professional changes
during my career. My college education prepared me to be a
professional in the YMCA, a career I followed for nearly ten
years. In my mid-thirties, I moved into industry, where I
pursued a career as a training specialist and training manager
for another ten years. Following that, I moved out on my own
as a professional speaker and management consultant/trainer,
a career I am still following today.

Many other illustrations could be shown. For example, one
of my colleagues started out as a human resources specialist in
a major corporation after college, moved into full-time consulting where he became a principal in a professional services firm,
and then moved back into the corporate world as Executive
Vice President of one of his client companies when they "made
him an offer he couldn't refuse." This is not an unusual pattern
for professionals. Keeping an open mind to future opportuni-

ties while broadening your experience base may accelerate your professional growth in unanticipated ways.

Creating and taking advantage of opportunities is generally much more productive if we keep our peripheral vision open. As that great philosopher, A. Nonymous, once said "Luck occurs when preparation meets opportunity." These "opportunities" are not limited to our profession. They can include such things as financial investments, real and personal property, family and friends, or anything that has a significant meaning in our lives. While there is always a risk in looking at opportunities, that risk tends to be reduced when we have anticipated it and planned how to deal with it.

Strategic planning can reduce the risk and significantly enhance our personal and business **security and safety.** This includes, of course, financial security, health, family well-being, and any other factors that might cause significant future trauma. You need to determine what is an appropriate balance between risk and security as you chart your future.

The subject of **retirement** can arouse a variety of different emotions, depending on where we are in both our chronological and professional lives. For many professionals, total retirement may never be a reality. The base and focus of our efforts may change significantly, but many of us *plan* to continue to be involved in practicing our professions to some degree as long as we are able. There are other professionals, however, who look forward to retirement for a significant change in lifestyle that will create new experiences that their careers may have interfered with in the past. My personal choice, since I enjoy and am creatively stimulated by what I do professionally, is to continue in that practice for the foreseeable future, although I may modify the pace somewhat. Regardless of where you happen to be in terms of your own perspective on retirement, when you come to the point where it is appropriate for you to back off from what you have been doing, it will be much more satisfying and fulfilling if it comes as a result of planned effort rather than the closing of a door.

Building and maintaining a **balanced life** is another significant benefit of personal strategic planning. Oftentimes, we, as practicing professionals, develop "tunnel vision" which keeps us narrowly focused on our business and careers. During certain periods of our lives, this may be justified. However, life is much more than getting ahead professionally or in business. We need to achieve a balance that includes family and friends, health and wellness, personal fulfillment that may not directly relate to our profession, financial planning, spiritual development, and service to others. Just as a chair will not function properly if one of its legs is longer or shorter than the others, neither will our lives function effectively without some overall balance. Giving significant attention to another important aspect of our lives does not necessarily detract from our professional focus. In fact, it is possible to achieve a true synergy wherein the "whole" person can be even more productive both professionally and personally.

A final significant benefit is the **opportunity to involve others** in making our futures come alive. These could include our life partners, parents and siblings, children, professional colleagues, employers, and friends who have either a vested interest in our success or a genuine concern about our future well-being. Since there are very few things in our lives that we can accomplish without the help of others, it is both sensible and desirable to get them involved as early as possible in the planning process. Not only are they able to offer significant contributions that may help to make our plans more effective, their active support in the pursuit of these efforts can go a long way toward assuring the achievement of these plans.

What Are Some Concerns We, as Professionals, Have with Personal Strategic Planning?

Dealing with the (apparent) conflict of **thinking versus action** frequently provides an interesting dilemma for professionals. We tend to be action-oriented. When we are doing something, we feel we are being productive. But, when we take the time to think, we sometimes feel guilty of being unproductive. In reality very little action occurs without realistic thinking – it is not "either-or," it is "both-and." In fact, without investing the time and effort required to think about where we are going, there is a very strong likelihood that we will never get there. Of course, we have to decide where "there" is, and it is difficult to do that without thinking about it.

The **time required** to do it can be a barrier to effective planning. How often have we said "I just haven't got the time to do that right now." While that may be a legitimate reaction occasionally, in many cases it turns out to be just an excuse. We frequently don't believe we have the time to plan the job sufficiently in advance but, when the job doesn't get done right, somehow or other we usually find the time to do it over again. Time is one of those exhaustible commodities with which we have to deal as professionals. Consequently, the planning process, while it does take time, could lead us to much more productive use of the limited time we do have available.

The use of **business jargon** sometimes gets in the way of professionals accepting the need for effective planning. Some people who are writing about planning seem to feel that one of the contributions they have to make is to invent new words that we "common folk" won't understand; therefore, we will have to come to them for guidance. While there are certain terms that have to be used in describing the planning process, there is no reason why most terms cannot be expressed in everyday language. We may then find less resistance on the part of people participating in the planning process. The *process* is what is important, not what the process is called. Whenever a label gets in the way of a process, change the label, not the process. (The intent in this book is to keep jargon to an absolute minimum. Also, if you have another term you use to describe the particular step in the process being discussed, then make a mental substitution for the one found here.)

Putting plans in writing is an action that many of us resist. (I must confess that, without the insistence of my wife and some of my colleagues that I need to "practice what I preach," I would tend to avoid it also.) *Writing something down is one of the first steps to making a commitment.* It does not have to be a lengthy document. Morrisey's Law says "the utility of any planning document is in inverse relationship to its length." The longer a planning document is, the less likely it is to be used effectively. Typically, the most frequently used planning document, whether in personal or business life, is a single sheet of paper. (The focus in this book will be to keep the amount of paperwork involved in your planning efforts down to an absolute minimum.)

The judgment we have to make is whether or not that one piece of paper is going to help move us in the desired direction better than without it. Much of the planning *process* can be handled through thinking and discussion. Those things that should be put in writing are ones that we will clearly need to refer back to in order to help us stay on course. For example, the writing of this book moved ahead much more rapidly and purposefully once I established a written schedule for chapter completion. The primary purpose of a written plan is to help offset our too-often faulty memories. But always remember that plans are a means to an end, never an end in themselves.

Changing circumstances is frequently given as a reason for not putting any significant effort into planning. "How can we plan when things are changing so fast!" As identified earlier, change or modification of plans is inevitable and, in many situations, is actually desirable. The key, of course, is to recognize when changes are taking place.

Many times we have started down a particular path toward a significant accomplishment only to be distracted by something that causes us to move in a different direction. Consequently, when obstructions intrude themselves upon us, we tend to respond with a "knee jerk reaction" resulting in our doing the *urgent* rather than the *important*. But with a plan, we can better determine when it is appropriate to deviate from that plan in a highly dynamic situation. There is nothing wrong with changing direction, provided we know we *are* changing direction and there is a valid reason for doing so. Therefore, in many situations, the purpose of a plan is to provide us with a foundation from which we can make appropriate and productive digressions.

The time **when things are going well** is when it is easy to fall into the trap of thinking that they will continue to go well "forever." This is probably the time when strategic planning is most critical. Despite the euphoria we may feel then, it is absolutely certain that it will not go on "forever." Something will happen that will be other than what we had hoped was going to happen, thus moving us, whether we like it or not, in a different direction. One of the single most important reasons for doing strategic planning is to be better prepared for dealing with those situations that may run counter to our desired direction. While we may not be able to anticipate everything that will impact our future, we stand a much better chance of dealing with it effectively if we have looked ahead and anticipated some of the things we might be facing.

When things are not going well, there is probably a more legitimate reason for postponing strategic planning efforts. When your house is on fire is not the time to think about installing a sprinkler system. When faced with survival, dealing with that has to take precedence, for, as one wag said, "In the long run we are all dead." The problem that frequently faces us, however, is that we seem to be always in a crisis situation. Unfortunately, these crises frequently come as a result of a lack of effective planning in the first place. If you find yourself in a situation where you seem to be moving from one crisis to another on a continuing basis, perhaps that is when you need to take some time off, sit back and really think about where it is that you want to go.

Finally, **not recognizing the difference** between strategic (or long term) and operational (or short term) planning may inhibit our efforts. Operational planning, which is commonly what we have to apply in dealing with crisis situations or in achieving short term results, tends to be quite specific and action-oriented. Strategic planning, on the other hand, tends to be conceptual and visionary. It has to do with direction rather than specific action. It is virtually impossible, in my judgment, to do strategic and operational planning at the same time. When faced with concerns that affect where we will be going in three to five years at the same time we are addressing what's going to happen next month, guess which one is going to get the most attention!

If you plan to commit yourself to some form of strategic

planning in your personal and professional life, it needs to be addressed when there is time for that to be the principal focus. As we will discuss later, you may find it helpful to have someone else assist you in the process who can keep you focused on the strategic or long term concerns. Think of strategic planning as helping you determine *where* it is you are going and operational planning as *how* you will get there.

Who Else Needs to be Involved?

No one can operate in complete isolation when it comes to the achievement of one's professional goals. We're all dependent, to varying degrees, on the help and support of other people. As was mentioned earlier, enlisting the support of those who are important to you early in your planning efforts can have tremendous payoff in terms of your personal satisfaction, the building of truly effective relationships, and the more rapid achievement of your goals. Most people are flattered to be included in your planning efforts. Furthermore, by including others, you can take advantage of many contributions they might make towards helping you get to where you want to go. Of course, this also suggests that you may need to play a role in helping them achieve what is meaningful for them. The fascinating thing about the strategic planning process, as we work with others who are important to us, is that it enables us to achieve a win-win kind of relationship. It does not have to be competitive. We will have considerably more to say about the role others may play in your planning as we proceed through this book.

How about a Strategic Planning Notebook?

As you get ready to move ahead with establishing your own strategic plan, I strongly recommend that you get a three ring binder and insert copies of the worksheets you intend to complete and the documents that flow out of them. In that way, you can make this a living process that will work for you which you can add to, modify and eliminate as fits your need.

In Summary

Strategic planning is accepted as an essential part of any business. What more important business do you have than the pursuit of your own professional career and personal life! The benefits of personal strategic planning covered in this chapter include: a personal vision for the future, a clear career direction, the creation of opportunities, the enhancement of security and safety, preparation for retirement, the building and maintenance of a balanced life, and the opportunity to involve others in making your future come alive. The concepts and techniques in this book are designed to help you create your own future. Get ready now to establish your own strategic plan and make it happen.

CHAPTER 2
Determining Your Professional Direction

A S YOU BEGIN TO FORMULATE your personal strategic plan, you need to make some choices. The first is to consider the various professional career options you have, both now and in the future. If you have already made a clear choice as to the direction you wish to follow, this may only require you to do some refining and clarification, although you still may wish to examine possible alternatives. If you are not completely certain as to the appropriate professional direction for you, here is an opportunity to explore some options, making a judgment as to which are at least worthy of your consideration.

What Are Your Professional Career Options?

I see three primary options that many professionals examine at some time during their careers, with several variations possible within each. These three are:

● Professional employee within a diversified organization
● Self-employed professional
● Professional within a professional services firm

For many professionals, it is possible, often even desirable, to be involved in more than one of these careers at the same time. Also, it is not unusual to move from one to another and back again. For example, an electronics engineer I know spent her first seven years after college working in two different electronics firms, the next four years as a self-employed contract engineer, and then went to work as a product line manager in a start-up company.

Because of my personal experience, the emphasis in this book will focus more on the professional who either is self-employed now or would like to be. This is not to suggest that any of the other options are less desirable or have less opportunity. Nor should you draw the conclusion that being self-employed does not have its share of frustrations. Being aware of what is involved in pursuing each of these options, however, makes for a better informed decision-making process.

Let's examine each of these three primary options and some of the considerations within each, recognizing that some may be more viable at one point in your career than at another.

For the Professional Employee within a Diversified Organization

Most professionals start out as an employee within an organization whose primary business is something other than providing professional services. For example: an engineer/scientist working in a high-tech manufacturing firm; an accounting/financial professional in a retail operation; a computer programmer/analyst in a government agency; a personnel specialist/trainer in a service business; a psychologist/social worker in a non-profit community agency. Even attorneys and physicians sometimes prefer employment within a firm, initially or permanently. The advantage to starting your professional career in this manner is that it provides an opportunity to build an experience base without necessarily committing yourself to a permanent career within that industry or organization.

You may even discover, as many have, that a *change* in your profession will become meaningful at some point. Employment in a professional position within an organization provides substantial flexibility, including a reasonable amount of financial security, while you hone your skills, evaluate whether or not this is the "right" profession for you, and determine what will be your most fulfilling future direction. Let's examine briefly some of those future options.

Continued employment as an internal professional within the same or, possibly, a different organization. This has appeal for many professionals because, while continuing to expand their capabilities and build their personal financial reserves, it provides them with the opportunity to work on increasingly challenging assignments, have access to professional resources that might not be as readily available elsewhere, and enjoy the collegiality of being with other professionals with common interests.

Moving into management. This is a logical career move for many people who start out as practicing professionals. Taking on the role of supervising other professionals, helping them expand their professional capabilities, and becoming a part of the decision-making hierarchy can be a very fulfilling and natural move. Also, the financial rewards of being a part of management tend to be greater, though not necessarily so. Unfortunately, many professionals who choose this career course fail to recognize the potentially traumatic circumstances that may accompany such a move.

Ironically, superior technical competence, a factor that usually gets the greatest consideration in initial managerial selection, may actually work to the disadvantage of both the organization and the professional. Professionals with superior technical ability often have a relatively low tolerance for other professionals who are not as skilled as they are. This, of course, would describe most of the people they have to supervise. Consequently, the temptation is to take on the more challenging technical projects personally because they know they can do them better than most of those who report to them. They tend to think of themselves, at least during the early time of their shift into management as, first and foremost an engineer, salesperson, accountant, or trainer *who also does some management work.* As a result, when such a manager is faced with a choice between making a technical or managerial decision, the technical effort usually receives preferential treatment. The problem with that, of course, is that the higher one moves in management, the more frustrated the true technical professional is likely to become.

At some point, in order to retain one's sanity, the individual has to recognize that he or she has changed professions. When we realize that we are now, first and foremost, *managers* who may, on occasion, do some technical work, then we can be more fulfilled in our jobs. Some professionals are able to make this transition fairly easily while others sometimes end up hating their jobs and the organization that has thrust them into such an uncomfortable position. While, presumably, such a professional always has the option of moving back into a pure technical role, this generally creates a situation that many people find untenable.

If movement into professional management has some appeal for you, the strategic planning process can help you identify some of the mental adjustments you will have to make and some of the expertise you may need to acquire.

Preparing to become an independent, self-employed professional. If you are like many professionals, you have dreamt, at some point, of eventually establishing your own independent professional practice. Perhaps you see employment within an organization as a legitimate way to prepare yourself for that eventuality. Not everyone who has such a dream will see it fulfilled. Economic realities and other considerations may cause the abandonment of that journey before it can be realized. The strategic planning process can help you identify those factors that need to be considered before making such a move.

For example, I decided, after about two years into my second career as a management trainer, to move toward positioning myself for full-time consulting. I originally set four years as my target. It took me eight. However, that time gave me an opportunity to accomplish several things that helped position me more effectively in the marketplace. I made two job changes after I determined the direction in which I wanted to go. These moves were designed to provide me with a broader experience base than I had had previously. My first significant training job was with North American Aviation (now Rockwell International) during the development of the Apollo program. I functioned as a management development specialist working primarily in a *research and development* environment. This provided me with the opportunity to develop my knowledge and skill as a trainer and to learn how to work effectively with managers in that kind of a setting. My next position was as Supervisor of Management Training at the Douglas Aircraft Co. There I was able to get experience as both a manager within my chosen profession and a trainer in a largely *production* environment, since I was a working supervisor.

My final move, before going out on my own, was as Manager of the West Coast Center for the Postal Service Management Institute. Perhaps surprisingly, this was the most entrepreneurial job I ever held. I had the opportunity to start up the first decentralized management training center in the Postal Service's history. Here I was able to acquire a middle management experience with a start-up operation in a service industry within a *governmental* environment. My strategic efforts also led to the publication of my first three books and to some other types of experience on my own which helped position me in my chosen profession.

Moonlighting while fully employed. Many professionals find it possible, practical and desirable to do some outside work, in addition to their regular jobs, as a vehicle for further professional preparation. In fact, many organizations encourage their employees to pursue such opportunities with the view that this will make them more effective in the long-run. Such opportunities could include teaching at a local university or college, working part-time in the evenings with a professional firm, taking on individual assignments that can be completed at home, or some other such pursuit which might enable you to practice your professional specialty in a distinctly different environment. In my own case, I taught several management courses in the evening at various community colleges and a state university. I also worked as a subcontractor for another management consultant, conducting workshops for some of his clients during the evening hours. In addition to providing more income, such activities can help broaden your perspective, and provide a useful experience which can be helpful in the future.

Preparing for retirement. Particularly if you plan to continue as a professional employee within an organization, strategic planning can be used effectively to prepare you for the time when full-time employment may not be possible or desirable. This, of course, includes financial planning for that time when a regular paycheck will not be coming in.

However, planning for retirement needs to include much more than financial planning. The advantage of many professions is that it is frequently possible to continue practicing even after formal retirement from an organization. This can include part- or full-time employment of the kind we have already discussed, volunteer work, writing, teaching, and a variety of other situations where your professional abilities can be put to productive use. It may also be appropriate for you to move into a different line of work, possibly opening a small business or even pursuing a different profession such as real estate, investments, or professional association leadership. Unfortunately, many professionals become so committed to their regular jobs that retirement creates a void that is almost impossible to fill. While this cannot be completely counterbalanced, the strategic planning process can help to identify and prepare you for a productive change in lifestyle.

For the Independent, Self-Employed Professional

If you either are now or are strongly considering becoming an independent professional, let's examine some important factors.

If you are just *starting out*, whether directly upon completion of your education or after having made the move from professional employment within an organization, there are five major considerations: capability, credibility, marketing/sales, financial resources, and business practices. Of these, **capability** may be the *least* important. I assume that, if you have made the decision to form your own professional services business, you have the requisite knowledge and skill to perform effectively within your chosen professional discipline. Regrettably, however, there are many highly capable people who have had disastrous experiences in trying to make it on their own; failure to give adequate consideration to one or more of the four other considerations is the usual cause of this.

Credibility is a more critical consideration for the independent professional than it is for someone employed within an organization. That which sets you apart from others, and gives you the right to perform critical professional services, becomes an important factor in entering the marketplace. In my role as a management consultant, I receive several letters or calls each month from professionals who, though having just completed their education, have decided to share their expertise with the world as consultants. While commendable, college degrees (even an MBA or PhD) do not necessarily establish a person as one who deserves to be paid independently for his or her professional services.

In my own case, I chose publication as the vehicle to establish my credibility. The three books I had published by the time I finally went independent set me apart from many of my colleagues who were also interested in pursuing that kind of a career direction. If publishing is not yet possible for you, the types of projects and the kinds of organizations with which you have worked can help provide credibility. Potential clients generally want to know for whom you have provided similar services in the past (which could be former employers as well as clients) and *what specific results came from your efforts*. The fact that you have worked for a period of time as a professional within an organization carries very little weight of itself, unless it can be backed up with significant accomplishments. Your strategic plan must address how your credibility can best be established.

Marketing/sales, like it or not, are essential skills for anyone who wants to make a living as an independent professional. The old cliché about "build a better mouse trap and the world will beat a path to your door" is utter nonsense. Potential clients do not, by and large, go looking for professionals that can assist them, unless they are in trouble. When that occurs, they are far more likely to look for someone who has been functioning as an independent professional long enough to have established a reputation. This means that, if you are starting out, you will probably spend significantly more time and effort in *getting* potential clients to buy your services than you will spend in providing those same services. (I will have more to say about marketing and sales responsibilities later in this book.)

Financial resources becomes a critical consideration for independent professionals who are starting out since it is highly unusual for such a person to produce sufficient revenue to cover his or her financial requirements during the first year or two of practice. Having sufficient financial resources available to cover start-up costs, capital outlays, operating expenses, and personal living expenses is an essential ingredient to getting a professional practice off the ground. Let's face it! How effective will you be in providing services to your clients if you have a major concern about whether you can pay the rent, meet your car payments, or put food on the table?

There are many ways, of course, that such financial resources may be acquired: accumulated savings, your spouse's income, an inheritance, income or equity from investments, borrowed funds, etc. The point is that your planning efforts clearly have to identify both financial requirements (they will generally be much higher than you think) and the resources that are available to you. Unfortunately, there have been too many independent professionals who, because of insufficient consideration to financial resources during their planning efforts, have had to give up their dreams of private practice and go back to seeking employment, just when they were on the brink of breaking through.

Business practices frequently end up being the undoing of many otherwise competent independent professionals. Insufficient attention to such things as bookkeeping, office management, clerical support, legal advice, and record-keeping can make a nightmare out of the operation of a professional practice. Yet many professionals either are not very good at or don't like to do these things. How the business side of your operation is handled is as important as is the practice of your professional specialty itself. Your plan has to take into consideration whether you will do this yourself, get assistance from your spouse, hire one or more employees to perform such duties, or seek assistance from service firms.

If you are a *mid-career* independent professional, presumably you have satisfied most of the concerns related to a start-up situation. Typically, you will be someone who has been a practicing independent for several years, has established a satisfactory client base and may be looking for ways to diversify. Your personal values may have changed somewhat since the early stages of your career. It may now be time to focus on things which may have received less attention earlier. Professionally, this could include raising the nature and scope of the professional practice to a higher level, moving into a different market, adding or expanding staff, introducing new services, or expanding your capabilities.

On the personal side, you may be looking for ways of giving more attention to your spouse or family, putting additional effort into financial investments, or exploring hobbies or other personal interests more seriously than was possible before. Again, the strategic planning process can help provide focus on where your effort should be directed.

If you are a *mature* independent professional, you may be approaching the time when you want to reduce your personal involvement in the business. This could include preparing to turn the business over to other family members, getting another professional to assume greater responsibility for running the business (thus enabling you to spend less time in its daily operations), preparing to sell the practice, establishing methods for generating more passive income, or just preparing to cut back on the effort required to maintain the practice with a view to its eventual dissolution.

You will probably have more options in private practice than if you are retiring from employment within an organization. In my own case, my wife and I decided to simplify our operation a few years ago when our secretary retired. We did not replace her with another employee but divided the workload and responsibilities between us. It has given us a much greater sense of freedom. I can continue to operate my practice at a level that is satisfying, without worrying about meeting a financial "nut" every month.

For the Professional within a Professional Services Firm

Many professionals such as accountants, attorneys and architects, will become affiliated with a professional firm within their discipline at some point during their careers. While many individuals will remain members of a professional firm for the rest of their careers, most entering such a relationship have one of three objectives in mind: to become a partner or principal in that firm, start their own firm, or position themselves for a high level professional or managerial position within another organization. Any one of these could be a worthwhile target for you to shoot for, but each will require a significantly different approach.

If **partnership within the firm** is your chosen direction, then such things as developing new business, creating additional services, establishing strong client relationships, and building the overall business of the firm become principal steps in your own strategic plan.

If moving towards **establishing your own professional practice** seems to have a greater appeal for you, then such things as expanding your knowledge, achieving personal certification (CPA or PE, for example), and learning the business side of the profession, while still serving the needs of your employer, become more crucial in your planning efforts. Most professional firms recognize that individuals starting out with them are not likely to stay forever. Therefore, the principals in that firm are often happy to provide appropriate advice and counsel to help you grow in your profession, with the expectation that they will receive a profitable service from you for only a relatively limited period.

If you see affiliation with a professional firm as a springboard to **employment with a broader-based organization**, where your expertise might be seen as a valuable commodity, you will probably want to place more emphasis on establishing your personal credibility (possibly including certification); also in developing a particular professional niche where you can excel, and in establishing a working relationship with certain client organizations who might be prospective future employers.

Being honest and above board with the principals in the professional firm in which you are employed can be a major step in moving you towards your ultimate destination. Regardless of which approach makes the most sense for you, the more effective a job of strategic planning you do, the greater the likelihood that you will be fully prepared to take advantage of opportunities as they come along.

Exercise – Getting Your Directional Focus

As you move ahead with your strategic plan, you need to narrow your options to those which have real potential from the standpoint of both your interests and capability. Take a look now at Figure 2.1, Your Career Path Options, as a vehicle for identifying where you are now and where you want to be in the future.

On the Checklist are several career positions along with six columns for your assessment of their desirability over time.

- "N.A." stands for "Not Applicable" and should be checked for any of the positions that clearly are not now nor would ever be likely to be something you would aspire to.
- "Am Now" means that is where you are currently in your career journey.
- "Do Now" represents a position you either will or should be moving into immediately, say within the next three months.
- "This Year" would cover a position to be attained within the next 12 months while "Next Year" or "Future" should be checked if either of them represents a more realistic time frame for you.

For some items, you may have a check in the "Do Now" and one or more of the three following columns. This would indicate that you need to begin preparing for it immediately, but do not expect to reach that position until some time in the future.

Figure 2.1: YOUR CAREER PATH OPTIONS

CAREER PATH	N.A.	Am Now	Do Now	This Year	Next Year	Future
Full time student						
Part time student						
Professional employee						
Manager						
Executive						
Private practice						
Professional firm staff						
Professional firm manager						
Professional firm principal/partner						
Educator						
Other						
Career change						

Use a check mark (√) for items that represent a firm position or a reasonable probability, and a question mark (?) if it is at least a distinct possibility, but one to which you are not yet ready to commit.

If you either are now a full or part time student or see either of these as appropriate positions for you at some point, put a check mark in the appropriate column(s), otherwise check them as "N.A."

A "professional employee" indicates that you are, or expect to be, working as a professional within a diversified organization where your primary responsibilities are of a professional or technical nature. You would check "manager" if your responsibilities, either now or in the future, include that of first line supervisor through middle manager. If your current or future responsibilities include both direct professional work and management, you would check both "professional employee" and "manager." "Executive" represents a position at or near the top of the organization, possibly as an officer, where you would have major decision-making responsibility.

"Private practice" is the line item you would focus on if you either are now, or expect to be, functioning as an independent, self-employed professional, practicing your craft either as an individual or in a firm in which you are the sole or majority owner.

If you see yourself working as a practicing professional within a professional services firm, then check "professional firm staff." Similarly, if you are now, or expect to be, functioning as a manager or principal/partner within such a firm, then check those items accordingly.

An "educator" is the line item to be assessed if being a full or part time faculty member is a part of your plan. Use the "other" line if you have identified a career objective that is not satisfactorily covered in any of the items above.

Finally, "career change" is something that should be identified if you plan to change either your profession or the organization within which you plan to practice your profession.

To illustrate the use of this checklist, please refer to Figure 2.2 where we will introduce Barbara Spangler, an electronics engineer, whom we will be following throughout the book. As you can see, she has checked both "student" categories, "educator," and "other" as not being applicable to her situation. As a project manager within her company, she sees herself primarily as a "professional employee" now with the intention of becoming a "manager" next year. Possibilities she wants to keep open for the future are: an "Executive" with her current employer, entering "private practice," and various levels within a professional services firm. She will also consider making a "career change" next year or in the future if progress with her current employer does not meet her expectations.

Figure 2.2: BARBARA SPANGLER'S CAREER PATH OPTIONS

CAREER PATH	N.A.	Am Now	Do Now	This Year	Next Year	Future
Full time student	√					
Part time student	√					
Professional employee		√				
Manager					√	
Executive						?
Private practice						?
Professional firm staff						?
Professional firm manager						?
Professional firm principal/partner						?
Educator	√					
Other	√					
Career change					?	?

In Figure 2.3, we introduce Jack Michaels, an accountant, whom we will also be visiting periodically throughout this book. The only items that he sees applying to him are "professional employee," which is currently his primary livelihood, and "private practice," which he is doing part time now during tax season, and is planning to move into full time next year when he anticipates receiving his CPA (which is why he has checked "career change").

If you have not done so already, take a few moments now to complete Figure 2.1 as it applies to you. (There is a blank copy in the Appendix if you would like to copy it for inclusion in

Figure 2.3: JACK MICHAEL'S CAREER PATH OPTIONS

CAREER PATH	N.A.	Am Now	Do Now	This Year	Next Year	Future
Full time student	√					
Part time student	√					
Professional employee		√				
Manager	√					
Executive	√					
Private practice		√			√	
Professional firm staff	√					
Professional firm manager	√					
Professional firm principal/partner	√					
Educator	√					
Other	√					
Career change					√	

your planning notebook.) I suggest that you use pencil initially as you may wish to make some changes later on.

In Summary

The first step in your strategic planning journey is to make some choices in terms of where you are now and where you might be heading on your career path. This will also help provide focus in terms of where you do *not* plan to go. In the next chapter, you will have an opportunity to assess those strategic *values* that will influence your future career-related decisions.

CHAPTER 3

Assessing Your Strategic Values

ONCE YOU HAVE SORTED THROUGH the professional choices you wish to consider, the next step is to assess those personal values that will affect your career decisions. As a guide to this assessment, I will adapt an approach developed in our book, *The Executive Guide to Strategic Planning*[1] which was, in turn, adapted from a book by Tregoe and Zimmerman entitled *Top Management Strategy: What It Is and How to Make It Work*[2]. The purpose of assessing values is to determine the relative importance of each, so as to identify your *driving force*, that *one* value which will ultimately determine your future career direction.

What Guides Your Professional Decision-Making Now?

How do you feel *now* when you are faced with making a critical future-oriented decision? Do you tend to make such decisions rationally, taking into consideration all relevant factors? Do you act without unnecessary delay? Have you generally been satisfied with the decisions you have made and with the results achieved from those decisions? If your decision-making thus far has been impulsive, dragged out, vacillating from one extreme to another, avoided, or clearly has not produced the desirable results, then you will find this chapter useful.

What Should Guide Your Decision-Making?

Some of the values that could or should influence your strategic thinking will be critical; others will have little or no importance to you personally; there may be still others that are especially important to you that do not appear on this list at all. Initially, don't be concerned about their relative importance. You will have an opportunity to prioritize them later in this chapter. At this stage, concentrate on understanding the potential impact of each, and let your mind run freely as you think of those values that are important to you.

Here are twelve strategic values we have identified that may be worth considering as part of your own strategic thinking in relation to your professional career. I will address these largely from the perspective of someone considering private practice. There is no significance in the order in which they are listed.

Independence/Freedom of Choice
Financial Return
Financial Security
Challenge/Risk Taking
Family Considerations
Geographical Focus
Service to Others
Personal Legacy/Estate
Professional/Peer Recognition
Professional Relationships
Power/Influence
Principles/Ethics

Lets examine each of these separately.

Independence/Freedom of Choice is frequently a value that attracts professionals into private practice. While we are employed within an organization, it is easy to become frustrated about situations over which we have no control. These include the types of projects to which we are assigned, working hours, working conditions, supervisory styles, or just the typical organizational bureaucracy. We begin to think "If I can just go into business for myself, I can do away with all this stuff." The desire to be one's own boss, for many, is a compelling reason for going into private practice.

While there is no doubt that the independent professional does have greater freedom of choice than most people employed within organizations, many who go into private practice quickly learn that the same frustrations exist, although with perhaps a different intensity. Working with a widely divergent group of clients can be frustrating as you learn to cope with their idiosyncracies. Also, if most of your work is with one or two major clients, you may find yourself in a situation that is not very different from the organizations where you were employed. Nevertheless, the degree to which independence is important to you will generally significantly influence decisions related to your future professional direction.

Financial Return must be considered. The prospect of increasing personal income, while at the same time being one's own boss, provides a decidedly attractive prospect for many professionals. While the potential for independent professionals to make significantly more money in private practice than was possible on salary within an organization is reasonably high, there are many professionals, particularly at the outset, who end up making less money with less benefits than they might have had if they had stayed employed, on salary, within an organization. Furthermore, there will be overhead expenses, previously covered by the employer, that will have to come out of gross revenue. As a rule of thumb, at least 50% more gross revenue than prior salary will be required for someone in private practice to be at the same income level.

Professionals need to recognize that achieving substantially higher financial return in private practice requires a significant investment of time and energy in attracting clients; experience indicates that clients rarely come looking for people who can provide them with professional services. Consequently, the career path of salary progression, incentive pay, and advancement within the organization should not be discarded lightly when making your critical career choices.

As an alternative, working within a professional services firm carries the potential of reasonable financial return with less risk than that associated with going into private practice. In addition, there is often the opportunity for earning incentive pay based on the amount of revenue personally produced, and the prospect of working toward becoming a partner or principal in the firm itself.

If you are contemplating going directly into private practice, the decision to move in that direction can be made with far greater confidence if you have a couple of "bread and butter clients" at the outset. Knowing that there is a modest amount of assured income to help underwrite the initial expense of opening a practice makes it easier to take that first big step.

My observation is that financial return is always a major factor to be considered before making future professional choices, but it is rarely the "driving force" that will be the single most important determining value.

Financial Security has a different focus than financial return. It concerns such matters as insuring a minimum level of monthly income to meet normal obligations; building a reserve for special expenses or investment opportunities; making certain that there will be sufficient financial resources available to take care of retirement.

One of the failings of many self-employed professionals is that they do not set aside sufficient money on a regular basis to take care of future requirements. If financial security is a major strategic value for you, you will probably feel more comfortable remaining on salary within an organization.

Challenge/Risk Taking can be an aphrodisiac for some professionals or anathema to others. Seeking challenge inevitably requires taking risks, which is why they are linked together here. There are opportunities for risk takers in all three of the major outlets for professionals (operating an independent practice, being part of a professional firm, working within an organization), but with different consequences for each.

The professional who works within an organization frequently has the opportunity to work on exciting, high risk projects. Partial or total failure on such projects is not likely to result in job loss unless that failure is truly catastrophic.

The risk of failure in a professional services firm is somewhat higher, particularly if it results in a significant loss of business.

The risk in independent practice is substantially higher from the standpoint of loss of revenue and credibility.

Looking at the positive consequences of risk taking, the potential for substantial return is higher for the independent professional than it is for someone working within a professional services firm or in another broad-based organization. Virtually every professional who thrives on risk taking has, at one time or another, seriously considered going into private practice. The degree to which risk taking is a positive or negative factor in your own strategic decision making should be considered in light of your need for personal security.

Family Considerations are often at or near the top of the list for many professionals. Those who are upwardly mobile in large organizations may be faced with the need to work regularly extended hours and, possibly, to relocate in order to achieve a desired position. Working within a professional services firm or as an independent professional can place similar demands upon the individual although they tend to be more at that individual's discretion. These demands are not always conducive to a close family relationship.

Each professional option presents opportunities for status and recognition that may appeal to some family members while serving as a deterrent to others. A professional who does not have the wholehearted support of his or her life partner will be at a distinct disadvantage in terms of achieving success and personal satisfaction. Therefore, a frank extended discussion of personal values that each has needs to be given major consideration when making a career choice.

Geographical Focus is important for some people. As indicated above, moving to a preferred location may be a real career benefit. However, if this requires your spouse to make some undesirable changes in his or her own career, it may prove to be an insurmountable obstacle. Also, particularly as an independent professional or one working within a professional services firm, your personal preference, or reluctance, for serving local as opposed to national or international clients may present major challenges related to the type of business you want to get involved in and the kinds of projects you wish to take on. While national and international travel can be exciting and rewarding, it can also become very tiring and frustrating, and a strain on family relations. While geographical focus is not likely to be your "driving force," it will need attention as you determine your future direction.

Service to Others is a value that leads many people to such professions as health care, social work, and education. The opportunity to make a difference in people's lives can be a powerful motivating force. However, there are ways to exercise this value in *all* professions. Having this as a strong personal value will influence your decisions on where you will work and what you will do during your non-working hours.

Personal Legacy/Estate refers to what you plan to leave behind, either broadly (to the world in general) or narrowly (to family and/or special interests), that will outlast your mortal existence. While this is frequently seen as representing material things such as money and property, it may include contributions you have made professionally that will have a lasting effect on others. The importance of this factor to you may influence the kinds of opportunites you wish to pursue.

Professional/Peer Recognition is a strong motivating force for many professionals. My own recognition in receiving the CPAE (Council of Peers Award of Excellence) from the National Speakers Association was an important milestone in my professional life. Other forms of certification and recognition, such as Certified Public Accountant, Chartered Life Underwriter, Certified Association Executive, Professional Engineer, Fellow, and a tenured professorship, represent achievements that are important to many professionals. Seeking opportunities that will enhance the likelihood of receiving such recognition may be an important consideration in charting your professional future.

Professional Relationships, the opportunity to interact and work collaboratively with other professionals whom you respect, is a strong need for many. This, generally, is more easily satisfied within a large organization. Professionals in private practice for whom this is an important value will have to look for other outlets, such as associations or informal network groups, where they can have the kind of collegiality they seek.

Power/Influence is an important value for those with hierarchical ambitions. The opportunity to control or significantly influence the direction of the organization, and the efforts of those employed there, is often the "driving force" behind rapid movement up the corporate ladder. While there are exceptions, people with power/influence as a high value will usually have more opportunities if they remain as part of a larger organization than will those pursuing other career options.

Principles/Ethics are very important factors for many professionals. Establishing and maintaining ethical or principle-based behavior presents many considerations regarding the type of business you wish to become involved in and the type of clients you wish to serve.

As you review the above list of potential strategic values, some additional ones may come to mind that play a significant role in your personal decision-making process. Remember, the purpose of assessing these critical strategic values is to help you identify and place in perspective the key factors necessary to make strategic decisions that will have a major impact on your professional and personal future.

How Do You Prioritize Your Own Strategic Values?

Please refer now to Figure 3.1, *Strategic Values Decision Matrix*. This is an analytical tool that can be used for taking a relatively large number of factors, to which a common set of criteria can be applied, and placing them automatically in rank order of importance. It is also a decision-making technique that can be used in a wide variety of other applications. (It is included in blank form in the Appendix.) However, we will use it here specifically as a vehicle for helping you place the strategic values that are important to you in rank order. You will note that we have listed the twelve strategic values described earlier in this chapter on the instrument itself.

The first step in using the tool is to go through the list and eliminate anything that does not significantly apply to your

Figure 3.1
STRATEGIC VALUES DECISION MATRIX

Column headers (1–14):

1. Independence/Freedom
2. Financial Return
3. Financial Security
4. Challenge/Risk Taking
5. Family Considerations
6. Geographical Focus
7. Service to Others
8. Personal Legacy/Estate
9. Professional/Peer Recog.
10. Professional Relationships
11. Power/Influence
12. Principles/Ethics
13.
14.

TOTAL "X'S"

Row labels:

1. Independence/Freedom
2. Financial Return
3. Financial Security
4. Challenge/Risk Taking
5. Family Considerations
6. Geographical Focus
7. Service to Others
8. Personal Legacy/Estate
9. Professional/Peer Recog.
10. Professional Relationships
11. Power/Influence
12. Principles/Ethics
13.
14.

Bottom grid (columns 1–14):

	1	2	3	4	5	6	7	8	9	10	11	12	13	14
VERTICAL (spaces)														
HORIZONTAL (X's)														
TOTAL														
RANK ORDER														

INSTRUCTIONS

1. Review list of strategic areas and eliminate any that do not apply to your situation; add any additional ones that may be appropriate on the blank lines, repeating each under the corresponding number at the top.

2. Evaluate #1 against #2. If #1 is more important, place "X" in box under #2; if #1 is less important, leave blank. Repeat with each remaining number. (Work only within the triangle of white boxes.) Continue to next line; repeat.

3. Total "X's" across for each number; enter in HORIZONTAL box at bottom; total "spaces" down for each number; enter in VERTICAL box at bottom; add both HORIZONTAL and VERTICAL for TOTAL.

4. Largest number under TOTAL will be #1 in RANK ORDER; next largest will be #2, etc. If two or more alternatives have the same TOTAL, RANK ORDER is determined by comparing each subjectively against the others.

own strategic planing. For example, if *Geographical Focus* is not an area that is of strong personal concern, you may choose to eliminate it.

Next, if you can identify additional factors that are important to you, they should be added to the list on the blank lines provided. For example, such things as *Family Involvement* (the opportunity to include your spouse or other family members in active roles within the business) or *Practice Availability* (the opportunity to enter or purchase an existing practice) may be appropriate to add to the active list.

You will notice that the vertical lines at the top of the matrix contain the same twelve factors listed on the horizontal lines. Therefore to make both sets consistent, you need to strike out any there that have been eliminated and include any that have been added so that both lists are identical.

Let me explain the process for completing the analysis first and then you can follow it in Figure 3.2 which represents an example of a completed analysis. This works under the principle of "paired comparisons" in which one item is compared to another and a decision is made as to which one is more important, according to the criteria presented. In other words, item 1, *Independence/Freedom of Choice* is compared to item 2, *Financial Return*, and a decision is made as to which one deserves greater consideration as you make your personal decisions on future career and business direction. If Independence is more important to you than Financial Return, you will place an "X" in the corresponding block where both are compared; if *Financial Reurn* is important leave the block blank.

Continue on as described in the instructions to Figure 3.1 until you have completed the tally in the bottom row (Rank Order). The item with the highest total in the Rank Order row will be your number one priority or "driving force," the item with the next highest total will be number two and so on.

Perhaps the easiest way to follow this decision-making process will be to refer to Figure 3.2, which represents the example of Barbara Spangler, the engineer who was introduced to you in Chapter 2. She is currently employed as a project manager within a large corporation. Barbara has determined that number 11, *Power/Influence*, is not of particular concern to her, so she has eliminated it from her list. However, an additional factor she wants to consider is the availability of an existing engineering consulting practice, with an established group of clients, where she can either purchase or earn a principal's position.

You will note that, as Barbara has compared item 1, *Independence/Freedom of Choice*, with each of the other vertical items, she has decided that Independence is *more* important to her than

Figure 3.2
STRATEGIC VALUES DECISION MATRIX
for Barbara Spangler
Electronics Engineer

	1 Independence/Freedom	2 Financial Return	3 Financial Security	4 Challenge/Risk Taking	5 Family Considerations	6 Geographical Focus	7 Service to Others	8 Personal Legacy/Estate	9 Professional/Peer Recog.	10 Professional Relationships	11 Power/Influence	12 Principles/Ethics	13 Practice Availability	14	TOTAL "X'S"
1 Independence/Freedom		X	X			X	X	X	X	X		X	X		9
2 Financial Return			X			X	X	X	X	X		X	X		8
3 Financial Security						X	X	X							3
4 Challenge/Risk Taking						X	X	X	X	X		X	X		7
5 Family Considerations						X	X	X	X	X		X	X		7
6 Geographical Focus							X								1
7 Service to Others															0
8 Personal Legacy/Estate															0
9 Professional/Peer Recog.										X					1
10 Professional Relationships															0
11 Power/Influence															—
12 Principles/Ethics															0
13 Practice Availability															0
14															

	1	2	3	4	5	6	7	8	9	10	11	12	13	14
VERTICAL (spaces)	0	0	0	3	4	0	0	2	4	4		6	7	
HORIZONTAL (X's)	9	8	3	7	7	1	0	0	1	0		0	0	
TOTAL	9	8	3	10	11	1	0	2	5	4		6	7	
RANK ORDER	3	4	9	2	1	11	12	10	7	8		6	5	

1. Family Considerations
2. Challenge/Risk Taking
3. Independence/Freedom
4. Financial Return
5. Practice Availability
6. Principles/Ethics
7. Professional/Peer Recog.
8. Professional Relationships
9. Financial Security
10. Personal Legacy/Estate
11. Geographical Focus
12. Service to Others

Financial Return, Financial Security, Geographical Focus, Service to Others, Personal Legacy/Estate, Professional/Peer Recognition, Professional Relationships, Principles/Ethics, and Practice Availability. She has decided that Independence is *less* important to her than Challenge/Risk Taking (she particularly enjoys working on projects with a high challenge) and Family Considerations (she is a single parent with two school-age children).

Figure 3.3
STRATEGIC VALUES DECISION MATRIX
for Jack Michaels Accountant

	1 Independence/Freedom	2 Financial Return	3 Financial Security	4 Challenge/Risk Taking	5 Family Considerations	6 Geographical Focus	7 Service to Others	8 Personal Legacy/Estate	9 Professional/Peer Recog.	10 Professional Relationships	11 Power/Influence	12 Principles/Ethics	13 Family Involvement	14	TOTAL "X'S"
1 Independence/Freedom		X	X	X	X	X	X	X	X	X	|	X	X		11
2 Financial Return			X	X	X	X	X	X	X	X	|	X	X		10
3 Financial Security				X		X		X		X	|	X			5
4 Challenge/Risk Taking								X			|				1
5 Family Considerations						X	X	X	X	X	|	X			6
6 Geographical Focus								X		X	|				2
7 Service to Others								X	X	X	|	X			4
8 Personal Legacy/Estate											|				0
9 Professional/Peer Recog.										X	|	X			2
10 Professional Relationships											|				0
11 Power/Influence	—	—	—	—	—	—	—	—	—	—	+	—	—	—	—
12 Principles/Ethics											|				0
13 Family Involvement											|				0
14											|				

	1	2	3	4	5	6	7	8	9	10	11	12	13	14
VERTICAL (spaces)	0	0	0	0	2	1	3	0	4	2	|	4	9	
HORIZONTAL (X's)	11	10	5	1	6	2	4	0	2	0	|	0	0	
TOTAL	11	10	5	1	8	3	7	0	6	2	|	4	9	
RANK ORDER	1	2	7	11	4	9	5	12	6	10	|	8	3	

1. Independence/Freedom
2. Financial Return
3. Family Involvement
4. Family Considerations
5. Service to Others
6. Professional/Peer Recog.
7. Financial Security
8. Principles/Ethics
9. Geographical Focus
10. Professional Relationships
11. Challenge/Risk Taking
12. Personal Legacy/Estate

Moving to line 2, *Financial Return* is more important to her than Financial Security and the rest of the items on the line with the exception of Challenge/Risk Taking and Family Considerations, for the same reasons identified above. Financial Security, on the other hand is less important to her personally than Professional/Peer Recognition, Professional Relationships, Principles/Ethics, and Practice Availability.

You can follow her decision-making process through the rest of the matrix with the rank order as tallied at the bottom. As it turns out, Family Considerations will be Barbara's "driving force" as she makes her future-oriented decisions with strong consideration being given to Challenge/Risk Taking, Independence/Freedom of Choice, Financial Return, and Practice Availability. Any change Barbara makes must be compatible with her family situation and should provide challenge, freedom of action and financial reward. Any shift into private practice will probably occur if and when she either purchases or earns a principal's position in an existing engineering consulting firm.

Let's look at another example. In Figure 3.3, we have Jack Michaels, our other Chapter 2 example, who is a senior accountant in a large retail organization. He feels he has reached a plateau in his current position and has no desire to move into a management role. He is currently preparing himself for the CPA examination. His wife, Linda, is an office manager in an insurance company who is attending school at night, working toward a business degree with a major in accounting. They have no children. He also has eliminated Power/Influence as a major consideration and has added Family Involvement, looking ahead to the possibility of establishing a business in which he and his wife might work together.

As you can see from Jack's analysis, Independence/Freedom of Choice turns out to be Jack's "driving force." Other major considerations include Financial Return, Family Involvement, Family Considerations, and Service to Others. Therefore, it would appear that Jack will be actively looking for opportunities, possibly after receiving his CPA, where he can operate independently with reasonably high potential for financial return and where there is a strong possibility of his wife eventually becoming a part of the business.

What Do You Need to Do to Change Your Strategic Direction?

If your analysis, through the Decision Matrix, indicates that a change in direction is appropriate, then you need to examine the implications of that shift, to identify specific issues. Answering the series of questions shown below may help you get that kind of focus. (There is a worksheet included in the Appendix entitled "Changing Your Strategic Direction" which covers these questions.)

1. What is my current driving force?
   Why has this been important?

2. What should be my future driving force?
   Why is that important?

3. What other major values need to be taken into consideration?

4. What changes need to be addressed to meet the requirements of my future driving force?

Let's briefly examine each of these questions as a means of getting a strategic focus.

1. What is my current driving force? Why is this important? You can probably make a quick assessment as to what your principal decision-making consideration has been up to the present time. If not, you may wish to go through the exercise again with current, rather than future, values as your criteria. You may reach the conclusion that what you have been following thus far is quite consistent with the direction in which you want to move. In that case, you probably will find it of little value to continue with this set of questions in order to get your strategic focus. On the other hand, if something is not consistent with where you want to go professionally, then following these questions may help determine changes you need to initiate.

For example, if Financial Security has been one of your major considerations until now and you see yourself with a strong personal motivation related to Independence/Freedom of Choice, you may find yourself faced with a significant dilemma. Try to make an objective assessment of what has guided your decision-making up until now, together with an evaluation as to why that has been important to you. This will help establish your *baseline* from which certain changes can be made.

2. What should be my future driving force? Why is that important? By articulating what you have now identified as your number one decision-making consideration for the future, you can begin to chart your course in terms of transitions that need to be made. For example, if Independence/Freedom of Choice is now your primary consideration, you need to objectively evaluate why you have reached that conclusion. Is it mostly because of dissatisfaction with your current position or is it because you really want to have the responsibility for making most of the business decisions that will affect your life? If it is the former, you may end up "jumping out of the frying pan into the fire." What are you willing to sacrifice in order to achieve true independence?

3. What other major factors need to be taken into consideration? Why is each of them important? Here is where you will list the other three or four major factors that you rated highly on your priority list. Even though your number one selection becomes your "driving force," these other high-ranking factors will also help shape your personal strategy. For example, if Financial Return and Family Considerations are high on your list of considerations although you have identified Independence/Freedom of Choice as your "driving force," you may need to look carefully at transitional moves before making your final decision to go into private practice.

4. What changes need to be addressed to meet the requirements of my future driving force? At this point, you should separate and articulate the specific targets and actions that need to be addressed when you set your Long Term Objectives and Strategic Action Plans. This should help you avoid making premature decisions that could prove disastrous. Once again, the illustrations shown below may prove helpful.

Figure 3.4: EXAMPLES OF STRATEGIC VALUE PRIORITIZATION

Barbara Spangler, Engineer

---

1. What is my current driving force? Why has this been important? My current driving force is Challenge/Risk Taking. One of the things that attracted me to the field of electronics engineering was the opportunity to push the state-of-the-art. My current job has provided me several opportunities to work on particularly challenging assignments.

2. What should be my future driving force? Why is that important? My driving force, for at least the next eight to ten years, has to be Family Considerations. When I was married, and even during the first two years following our divorce, my husband and I each spent a reasonable amount of time with the children. The six months since he has moved from the area have been a difficult transition for the children and for me. I realize now that my children mean more to me than my job and that I will have to make some adjustments in my priorities at least until they are both out of high school.

3. What other major factors need to be taken into consideration? Why is each of them important? Financial Return is especially important for the next several years, as I need to build up cash reserves both for my children's college education and to position me for other professional opportunities in the future. In my work, in addition to Challenge/Risk Taking, Independence/Freedom is high on my list. As long as I can maintain reasonable amounts of independence and freedom with my current employer, coupled with increased responsibility and reward, I will continue to work here. If both challenge and freedom erode in the future (after my family obligations have been fulfilled), I will be looking for other opportunities, possibly in private practice.

4. What changes need to be addressed to meet the requirements of my future driving force? I need to rearrange my work schedule so that I can plan my time for being with the children more predictably. (This can be done, but it requires some discipline on my part.) I will need to reach agreement with my supervisor and co-workers on how to adjust my schedule so that my family needs do not detract from on-the-job performance.

Jack Michaels, Accountant

---

1.   What is my current driving force? Why has this been important? Although not specifically identified previously, it is obvious that Financial Security has been my driving force for the past several years. I had become comfortable in my job until I decided to go for my CPA. This has opened up new vistas for me.

2.   What should be my future driving force? Why is this important? Independence/Freedom is clearly the factor that will have the greatest influence on any move to private practice. I want the opportunity to choose the kinds of work I will do and to make independent decisions on my future professional direction.

3.   What other major factors need to be taken into consideration? Why is each of them important? Financial Return has to be a major consideration both in preparing for going into private practice and for developing my clientele. Family Involvement is also a significant factor. My wife and I would like to be in business together. She is currently attending school at night, working toward a business degree with a major in accounting. That, together with the achievement of my CPA, should position us well for the future.

4.   What changes need to be addressed to meet the requirements of my future driving force?

   a. We will need to build additional cash reserves to support us at the time we make the move into private practice.

   b. I need to develop some knowledge of and skill in marketing and sales.

c. I need to develop a business plan prior to establishing my practice.

d. My wife may need to continue working at her current job until the practice is established.

Exercise – Assessing Your Strategic Values

If you have not done so already, complete the Decision Matrix following the instructions on pages 33–35. (There is another copy of this tool in the Appendix which you may feel free to duplicate for your own use, if you wish.) You may find it helpful to complete this with the assistance of your life partner, a colleague or a friend who can help keep you focused on the task at hand.

Next, complete the questions on the Appendix worksheet entitled "Changing Your Strategic Direction," which will lead to the identification of critical changes you need to implement. Be sure to make copies of these blank worksheets for inclusion in your Strategic Planning Notebook.

In Summary

Assessing your strategic values provides additional focus on how your future career decisions will be made. I have identified twelve strategic values, some or all of which will impact the future decision-making of any professional. They are: independence/freedom of choice, financial return, financial security, challenge/risk taking, family considerations, geographical focus, service to others, personal legacy/estate, professional/peer recognition, professional relationships, power/influence, and principles/ethics. There may be other values that are important to you. Through a process of forced ranking, using the tool I have called the Decision Matrix, you can determine the relative importance of each of these factors including your own personal "driving force" – that one factor which will be the ultimate determinant of your future courses of action. By keeping these priorities in mind, you will be able to identify and implement changes in your work and your life that will bring you much closer to personal fulfillment.

End Notes

[1] *The Executive Guide to Strategic Planning* by Patrick J. Below, George L. Morrisey and Betty L. Acomb, San Francisco: Jossey-Bass, 1987.
[2] *Top Management Strategy: What It Is and How to Make It Work* by Benjamin B. Tregoe and John W. Zimmerman, New York: Simon & Schuster, 1980.

CHAPTER 4

Preparing Your Personal and Professional Mission Statement

NOW THAT YOU HAVE NARROWED DOWN your professional career choices and made an assessment of the strategic values that will have the most impact on your future decisions, you are ready to move into the preparation of the first portion of your personal strategic plan — your personal and professional mission statement.

A statement of mission is probably the single most important strategic document you can have whether you are functioning as a Fortune 500 corporation, a small to medium size business, or as an individual professional. It establishes a firm foundation providing clear guidance for all significant decisions. A mission statement describes the nature and concept of your profession or business as well as the quality of life in which you expect to be involved. It also clarifies how decisions will be made regarding clients or employers you will be serving, services or products you will be providing, and, most importantly, the fundamental philosophy and values under which you expect to operate. In addition, it serves as a device for communicating with others who are important in your career and life.

What are the Benefits of a Personal and Professional Mission Statement?

A mission statement is not a static document. It is a dynamic, living thing that can provide all sorts of benefits. Let's examine some of these.

● It specifies the **specific kinds of business** in which you should be involved, thus providing a clear focus on where your energies should be directed. (I am interpreting the term "business" in the broadest sense, implying both the application of your professional skills and the type of organization within which these skills are applied.)

For example, suppose you are currently an engineer in a high-tech company with ambitions to move into a more responsible position. If you continue your focus within your engineering discipline, your managerial future is limited. If, however, you were to identify your future business role as "managing and integrating a multi-disciplinary operation," this might open up significant opportunities for expanding your horizons.

Or suppose you are an accountant who is currently in the business of providing bookkeeping services to small businesses. With that tight a focus, expansion can only come from adding additional clients. If, however, you see your future business as "providing financial advice, counsel, and record keeping services," this might open up opportunities in such things as income tax preparation, assistance in securing financing for a business, investment counseling, and personal and business financial planning.

If you are a computer programmer/analyst, either inside or outside a major organization, who identifies your business broadly as "systems design and support," you might provide services as widely varied as hardware and software acquisition, installation and integration, management information systems design or modification, systems education, time sharing services, or actual management, as a vendor, of systems operations for one or more separate businesses.

● A mission statement helps **determine what not to do,** to keep you from investing time, energy and other resources in activities that are inconsistent with your goals. For example, I determined mid-way in my consulting career that I was going to concentrate on providing only products and services that had been developed partially or entirely by me. Over the years I have had many opportunities to take on additional products or services, developed by others, some of which provided very attractive profit potential. Had I pursued those opportunities more diligently, however, it would have diverted me from my strategic plan which was to position myself as one of the top experts in my field.

● It helps in **communicating your philosophy and values** to others. Taking a clear position on such things as ethical or environmental issues, quality of service, relationships with clients, commitment to your family, and the role you intend to play in contributing to your profession can focus your efforts as well as help avoid future misunderstandings. For example, if one of your personal convictions is that you will not, knowingly, perform any professional action that will have a negative effect on the environment, stating that in your mission puts you on record to that effect for your own guidance as well as for the information of others.

● A mission helps to **create a professional image**. The fact that you have developed a statement of personal and professional mission, which is thoughtfully prepared and which you are, in fact, following, communicates very clearly to others, who may be in a position to support you, that you are really serious about your profession and are prepared to back up whatever you are committing yourself to do. This can be used with potential clients, associates, vendors, employers, bankers or venture capitalists, and professional colleagues.

How to Develop Your Personal and Professional Mission Statement

The first step is to seclude yourself where you can spend an hour or two completely uninterrupted and write down answers to questions such as those shown in Figure 4.1. You may wish to add to, delete or modify these questions based on personal preferences and the circumstances in which you find yourself.

These questions should also be answered by anyone else who has a strong vested interest in how you pursue your profession. These could include your spouse and/or other family members, business/professional associates, and close personal friends or advisors. I suggest that this be done independently at first to reduce the potential of being unduly influenced by the answers of others.

Next, arrange with someone who does *not* have a strong vested interest in its outcome to help you facilitate the development of your mission statement. (This could be a professional colleague with whom you might have a reciprocal arrangement; in other words that person helps you develop your statement of mission and you, in turn, help him or her.) The role of a facilitator is to force you to defend what you have stated and to help you identify any factors which may have been overlooked. This may include playing the role of "devil's advocate" on occasion.

When others are involved in helping you develop your statement of mission, the facilitator's job is to draw out divergent points of view with the aim of creating a true synergy. The statement that eventually emerges should end up being stronger and more meaningful than one developed on your own.

Figure 4.1: CLARIFYING YOUR PERSONAL AND
PROFESSIONAL MISSION

1a.   What business and/or profession *am* I in personally?

1b.   What business and/or profession *would I like* to be in? (What do I really enjoy?)

1c.   What business and/or profession *should* I be in?

2.   What is my basic purpose in business and in life?

3.   What are or should be my principal business functions and roles, present and future?

4.   What is unique or distinctive about what I can bring to my business/profession?

5.   Who are or should be my principal customers, clients, or users?

6. What are the principal market segments, present and future, in which I am most effective?

7. What is different about my personal business position from what it was three to five years ago?

8. What is likely to be different about my personal business position three to five years in the future?

9. What are my principal economic concerns?

10. What are or should be my principal sources of income?

11. What philosophical issues, personal values and priorities are important to my future?

13. What special considerations do I have in regard to the following (as applicable)?

- Board of directors or other outside group
- Employer(s)
- Partners or associates
- Staff
- Customers, clients, or users
- Vendors or suppliers
- Professional colleagues
- Professional associations
- Family
- Church or community
- Myself
- Other (specify)

Your statement of mission may not reflect all the answers to these questions and any others you may have identified. However, they all have strategic implications which may need to be addressed in other parts of your personal strategic plan. Perhaps more than in any other step in the entire plan, the *process* of developing a statement of mission is far more important than the *product*. The thought, discussion, evaluation, modification and reflection that take place during the development effort represents the primary value that comes from your statement of mission. The statement itself is merely a codification of the effort that you go through.

Examples of Personal and Professional Mission Statements

Following are some examples of how professionals answered the questions initially and how their mission statements evolved. The first two examples represent my own answers and mission statements as I actually completed them in 1990 as a full time speaker/trainer/consultant/author in a mature privately-owned company (Figures 4.2 and 4.4) and as I might have completed them in 1967 as a management training specialist at Rockwell International (Figures 4.3 and 4.5) While the two missions are compatible, notice the distinctly different focus in both business and values between my current circumstances and when I was in a mode of rapid career development.

The next example is Barbara Spangler, our electronics engineer with a PhD who, as a single parent, needs to balance her strong commitment to career and financial growth with maintaining a supporting and loving relationship with her children (Figures 4.6 and 4.7). Jack Michaels, our final example, is a senior accountant in a large retail organization who is working on achieving his CPA and would like to establish his own financial and accounting services practice where his wife can eventually join him (Figures 4.8 and 4.9).

Naturally, these are not, and should not be seen as, prescriptive responses for any professional. An attempt to copy even a modified version of one of these statements as your own would defeat the true value of the process.

Figure 4.2: CLARIFYING YOUR PERSONAL AND PROFESSIONAL MISSION **(for George Morrisey 1990)**

1a. What business and/or profession am I in personally?
  - Management and organizational planning education and facilitation – speaking, training, consulting, writing, training other consultants, production, sale and distribution of learning materials authored or coauthored by me
1b. What business and/or profession would I like to be in? (What do I really enjoy?)

- The same but with increased emphasis on speaking and the production, sale and distribution of learning materials

1c. What business and/or profession should I be in?
- See 1b.

2. What is my basic purpose in business and in life?
- To provide long-lasting, innovative, results-oriented management and planning concepts, processes and techniques for organizational leaders
- To contribute to the net worth and personal and professional growth of principals and associates in my business and to have fun while doing it

3. What are or should be my principal business functions and roles, present and future?
- Speaking to associations, corporations and government agencies on planning-related topics
- Designing and facilitating strategic and operational planning meetings and processes and consulting with executives on effective planning implementation
- Designing and conducting executive and middle management seminars and workshops on planning
- Writing/publishing management books, cassette learning programs and other publications on planning
- Marketing my speaking/consulting/training services and learning materials

4. What is unique or distinctive about what I can bring to my business/profession?
- High visibility through my published works and reputation as a professional speaker, consultant and seminar leader
- In-depth knowledge of and experience in the design and implementation of planning systems
- Products and services represent only works authored or coauthored by me

5. Who are or should be my principal customers, clients, or users?
- Senior executives in medium-sized organizations
- Association executives

- Human resource practitioners
6. What are the principal market segments, present and future, in which I am most effective?
    - Innovative, fast-growth companies
    - Federal, state and local government agencies
    - Divisions of major corporations
    - Selected trade and professional associations
7. What is different about my personal business position from what it was three to five years ago?
    - We are operating as a family business with only my wife and myself active in the company
    - I have two additional books published (for a total of fourteen) – prior to this book
    - I am doing more consulting/facilitating than training with some additional speaking
8. What is likely to be different about my personal business position three to five years in the future?
    - I will be reducing (but not eliminating) the amount of time spent in direct client services and increasing the amount of time spent in writing and publishing
    - Non-service income must increase 100-200%
    - Products offered must be state-of-the-art in content and packaging
9. What are my principal economic concerns?
    - Improving and maintaining cash flow and gross profit
    - Increasing "no sweat" income
    - Achieving and maintaining a comfortable life style
    - Building future residual income
    - Providing a modest estate
10. What are or should be my principal sources of income?
    - Fees for services
    - Program sales of products
    - Direct organizational and individual sales of products
    - Royalties from other publishers
    - Non-service fees, interest, investment distributions, etc.
11. What philosophical issues, personal values and priorities are important to my future?

- Continuing to provide high-quality, high-content services and products
- Maintaining the highest standards of ethical and professional conduct
- Being seen by my peers in the top echelon of our profession
- Contributing to the growth of my profession through volunteer leadership and assistance in the development of developing professionals
- Providing a stable family environment that will nurture the development of our grandchildren
- Providing volunteer leadership in our church and community

12. What special considerations do I have in regard to the following (as applicable)?
   - (None other than those identified above)

Figure 4.3: CLARIFYING YOUR PERSONAL AND PROFESSIONAL MISSION **(for George Morrisey in 1967)**

1a. What business and/or profession am I in personally?
   - Management training specialist in the aerospace industry (research and development focus)
1b. What business and/or profession would I like to be in? (What do I really enjoy?)
   - Management training supervisor in a production-oriented company (Phase 1)
   - Head of training function in a service or governmental operation (Phase 2)
   - Full-time independent self-employed management consultant/trainer (Phase 3)
1c. What business and/or profession should I be in?
   - Full-time independent management consultant/trainer; company owner
2. What is my basic purpose in business and in life?
   - To help individuals and organizations grow and prosper while achieving financial independence and to have fun while doing it

3. What are or should be my principal business functions and roles, present and future?
    - Designing, developing and conducting management training programs
    - Managing/supervising a training function
    - Marketing training/consulting services
    - Writing/publishing management books and other publications
4. What is unique or distinctive about what I can bring to my business/profession?
    - Strong analytical and people skills
    - In-depth knowledge of and experience in training methodologies and techniques
5. Who are or should be my principal customers, clients, or users?
    - Middle and first line managers in knowledge-based operations
    - Human resource practitioners
    - Corporate executives (future)
6. What are the principal market segments, present and future, in which I am most effective?
    - Aerospace and other high technology industries
    - Service and not-for-profit organizations
7. What is different about my personal business position from what it was three to five years ago?
    - I have changed professions from a professional/manager in a community service organization (YMCA) to that of a management training professional in industry.
8. What is likely to be different about my personal business position three to five years in the future?
    - I will be a published author.
    - I will be either managing a training function or in private practice as a full-time trainer/consultant
9. What are my principal economic concerns?
    - Sufficient cash flow to support my family
    - Sufficient reserves to launch my move into private practice

10. What are or should be my principal sources of income?
   - Salary from primary employer
   - Fees/wages from part-time training/consulting efforts
   - Royalties from books (future)
   - Income from investments (future)
11. What philosophical issues, personal values and priorities are important to my future?
   - To operate with the highest ethical and professional principles and standards
   - To become recognized as a leading authority in my field
   - To have a collegial relationship with other professionals in my field
   - To be in a business where my wife and I can work together
12. What special considerations do I have in regard to the following (as applicable)?
   - Board of directors or other outside group: Not applicable
   - Employer(s): To continue to give superior performance and high value while preparing for other opportunities
   - Partners or associates (future): To continually seek out and develop opportunities for mutually-beneficial personal and financial growth
   - Staff (future): To treat them as contributing partners in whatever business I may be involved in
   - Customers, clients, or users: To always provide high value regardless of contract arrangements and fees paid
   - Vendors or suppliers: To seek out and work with suppliers with similar values and to treat them as contributing partners
   - Professional colleagues: To establish and maintain relationships with other professional colleagues that result in mutual growth
   - Professional associations: To be active in a select few professional associations in which I can make a meaningful contribution and can achieve professional recognition

- Family: To maintain a loving and supporting relationship with my family regardless of business or professional developments
- Church or community: To be an active contributor, both financially and in service, to my church and community
- Myself: To continually challenge myself to grow in all aspects of my life
- Other (specify): Not applicable

Figure 4.4: GEORGE MORRISEY'S PERSONAL AND
PROFESSIONAL MISSION (1990)

My mission is to establish and maintain a balanced life encompassing a profitable business (which includes speaking, training, consulting and writing); to contribute to the state of the art in organizational and personal planning; to enrich my relationship with my family and my God; and to be of service to my church, community and profession. In support of this, I am committed to:

- continuing to provide high-quality, high-content services and products to my clients (as long as I am physically and mentally able) with increased emphasis on speaking, and production, sale and distribution of learning materials authored or co-authored by me.

- maintaining the highest standards of ethical and professional conduct.

- being seen by my peers in the top echelon of our profession.

- achieving and maintaining a comfortable life style that will enable my wife and me to enjoy life and each other for the foreseeable future.

- providing a stable family environment, in partnership with my wife, that will nurture the development of our grandchildren.

- contributing to the growth of our profession through volunteer leadership and assistance in the development of developing professionals.

- prviding volunteer leadership in our church and community.

- providing a modest estate.

Figure 4.5: GEORGE MORRISEY'S PERSONAL AND PROFESSIONAL MISSION (1967)

My mission is to continue to build a career in the training and development field leading to the formation of my own training/consulting services company. My purpose is to help individuals and organizations grow and prosper while achieving financial independence myself – and to have fun while doing it. In support of this, I am committed to:

- giving superior performance and high value to my current and future employer(s).

- providing high-quality, high-content training and development services to non-employer clients with whom I do business.

- writing and publishing books and training materials that will enable clients and readers to increase their effectiveness as managers and contributors to their organizations' objectives.

- becoming recognized as a leading authority in my field.

- operating in all areas with the highest ethical and professional principles and standards.

- maintaining a strong collegial relationship with other professionals in my field.

- strengthening relationships with my family, including the possibility of building a business where my wife and I can work together.

Figure 4.6: CLARIFYING YOUR PERSONAL AND PROFESSIONAL MISSION (Barbara Spangler, PhD, Electronics Engineer)

1a. What business and/or profession am I in personally?
- Project manager/engineer in a large, high technology corporation

1b. What business and/or profession would I like to be in? (What do I really enjoy?)
- Engineering management with increased responsibility and challenge
- Principal in an engineering consulting firm

1c. What business and/or profession should I be in?
- Engineering management with my current employer provided opportunities for increased responsibility and challenge are made available; otherwise with another employer or, possibly, with an existing engineering consulting firm where the opportunity to become a principal exists

2. What is my basic purpose in business and in life?
- To be able to provide a secure and loving home for my children while working in a highly challenging engineering management position that provides increasing opportunities for professional growth and financial return

3. What are or should be my principal business functions and roles, present and future?
- Designing and analyzing complex state-of-the art electronics systems
- Managing and coordinating the work of other skilled professionals in such projects

4. What is unique or distinctive about what I can bring to my business/profession?
- Superior design and analytical skills, supported by my PhD
- Ability to achieve superior results involving others with multi-disciplinary backgrounds

5. Who are or should be my principal customers, clients, or users?

- Program Managers overseeing complex state-of-the-art electronics systems
6. What are the principal market segments, present and future, in which I am most effective?
   - Large governmental agencies such as Department of Defense, Department of Energy and NASA
   - Prime government contractors
   - Large commercial electronics firms
7. What is different about my personal business position from what it was three to five years ago?
   - I now have project management responsibility in addition to individual design and analysis.
   - I am divorced with the responsibility for raising two school-age children.
8. What is likely to be different about my personal business position three to five years in the future?
   - I will have a higher level engineering management position in this or another company.
   - My children will both be in high school (freshman and junior years).
9. What are my principal economic concerns?
   - Increased cash flow
   - Increased cash reserves
10. What are or should be my principal sources of income?
    - Salary from employer
    - Performance bonuses from employer
    - Income from investments
11. What philosophical issues, personal values and priorities are important to my future?
    - To maintain a supporting and loving relationship with my children
    - To work on increasingly challenging engineering projects where I have significant autonomy
    - To be increasingly rewarded financially for my contributions
12. What special considerations do I have in regard to the following (as applicable)?
    - Board of directors or other outside group: Not applicable

- Employer(s): To provide consistently superior performance that will justify increased compensation
- Partners or associates: Not applicable
- Staff: To continually acknowledge and express appreciation for support received
- Customers, clients, or users: To provide consistently superior performance that will justify increased compensation from my employer
- Vendors or suppliers: To continually acknowledge and express appreciation for support received
- Professional colleagues: To maintain a collegial relationship while continuing to strive for superior performance
- Professional associations: To use my membership as a means for increasing my knowledge, skill and worth to my employer
- Family: To help my children grow as maturing youth so they can achieve independence and fulfillment when they reach adulthood
- Church or community: To be a responsible member of my community
- Myself: To continue to grow as a responsible parent and professional
- Other (specify): Not applicable

Figure 4.7: BARBARA SPANGLER'S PERSONAL AND
PROFESSIONAL MISSION

My mission is to provide a secure and loving home for my children while working in a highly challenging engineering management position that provides increasing opportunities for professional growth and financial return. In support of this, I am committed to:

- maintaining a supporting and loving relationship with my children.

- providing superior performance to my employer while

working on increasingly challenging projects where I have significant autonomy.

- exercising leadership in achieving superior results involving other professionals with multi-disciplinary backgrounds.

- seeking opportunities, with my current employer or with others, where my talents in engineering and engineering management can be fully utilized and where I can be increasingly rewarded financially for my contributions.

Figure 4.8: CLARIFYING YOUR PERSONAL AND PROFESSIONAL MISSION (Jack Michaels, Accountant)

1a. What business and/or profession am I in personally?
   - Senior accountant in a large retail organization
   - Part time tax preparer
1b. What business and/or profession would I like to be in? (What do I really enjoy?)
   - Outside accounting firm
   - Private accounting practice
   - Family owned business with my wife
1c. What business and/or profession should I be in?
   - Family owned private accounting practice with my wife
2. What is my basic purpose in business and in life?
   - To be able to provide superior financial and accounting services in an environment that enables me to work independently with the prospect of strong financial return; and to strengthen the relationship with my wife leading to personal fulfillment for each of us
3. What are or should be my principal business functions and roles, present and future?
   - Providing business and personal accounting services
   - Providing financial planning and investment counseling services to businesses and individuals

- Marketing these services to businesses and individuals
4. What is unique or distinctive about what I can bring to my business/profession?
  - Ten years of responsible accounting experience in retail operations
  - Continuing education in business and accounting with prospect of achieving CPA in the near future
5. Who are or should be my principal customers, clients, or users?
  - Chief Executive Officers and Chief Financial Officers in small to medium sized businesses
  - Individuals or families with income in upper middle income bracketrs
6. What are the principal market segments, present and future, in which I am most effective?
  - Small to medium sized retail and service businesses within a twenty-five mile radius of our location
  - Selected retail operations outside that radius
7. What is different about my personal business position from what it was three to five years ago?
  - I have reached a plateau in my current position since I have no desire to move into a management role. I am preparing for the CPA examination and expect to pass.
  - My wife is an office manager in an insurance company who is attending school at night, working toward a business degree with a major in accounting.
8. What is likely to be different about my personal business position three to five years in the future?
  - I will have my CPA.
  - My wife will have completed her degree.
  - We will be in business together.
9. What are my principal economic concerns?
  - Sufficient cash flow to maintain our current life style
  - Sufficient cash reserves to enable us to start our own private practice
10. What are or should be my principal sources of income?
  - My wife's and my current salaries from our employers
  - Fees from tax preparation clients

- Retainer fees from client businesses (future)
- Fees for specific financial and accounting services (future)

11. What philosophical issues, personal values and priorities are important to my future?
    - To operate independently where my income is directly commensurate with my skills and abilities
    - To be able to work with my wife in a business relationship that will strengthen our marriage
    - To maintain the highest professional and ethical standards in my dealings with clients

12. What special considerations do I have in regard to the following (as applicable)?
    - Board of directors or other outside group: Not applicable
    - Employer(s): To continue to provide quality service while positioning myself to move into private practice
    - Partners or associates: Not applicable
    - Staff: To work with them toward the fulfillment of their own career goals
    - Customers, clients, or users: To be sensitive to their needs and alert to opportunities to be of additional service
    - Vendors or suppliers: To treat them honestly and with respect
    - Professional colleagues: To maintain a cordial, professional relationship
    - Professional associations: To join and become active in associations that will support my business goals
    - Family: To continue to treat my wife as a full partner in both business and life
    - Church or community: To use my skills as a means of service to my church and community and also as a means of building lasting business relationships
    - Myself: To continue to improve my mind, body and spirit in all aspects of my life
    - Other (specify): Not applicable

Figure 4.9: JACK MICHAELS' PERSONAL AND PROFESSIONAL MISSION

My mission is to provide financial and accounting services in an environment that enables me to work independently with the prospect of strong financial return, and to strengthen the relationship with my wife leading to personal fulfillment for each of us. This will be accomplished through the formation of a private accounting practice, in which my wife and I can work together, with primary service to small and medium sized retail and service businesses and individuals in the upper middle income brackets. In support of this, I am committed to:

- achieving and maintaining the CPA designation.

- continuing to provide quality service to my employer while positioning myself to move into private practice.

- expanding my service capabilities to include financial planning and investment counseling.

- maintaining the highest professional and ethical standards in my relationships with clients.

- using my skills as a means of service to my church and community and also as a means of building lasting business relationships.

- continuing to improve my mind, body and spirit in all aspects of my life.

How to Make Your Mission Statement a Living Document

Once the initial draft of your mission statement has been developed, you may find it useful to circulate copies among some of your professional colleagues, family members or friends who can provide you with some meaningful feedback. Letting it simmer for several days can help identify other factors that ought to be included and suggest modifications that might strengthen the document itself.

You probably will not be completely satisfied with your initial draft or even with the modified one developed after feedback. However, I strongly recommend that you adopt your mission statement as representing your *current perspective* with the understanding that it can be reviewed and modified at a later date. You are far better off having an imperfect document, one that can at least get you started with the rest of your strategic planning effort, than waiting until you have one that ties up all the loose ends.

Your mission statement should be formally reviewed at least once a year, or whenever you are faced with a significant change in the nature of your business. With corporate clients, I recommend that they review their mission statements annually. It is generally a more valuable exercise to do this as though one was not already in existence, rather than attempting to do an editing job on the original document. An existing mission statement will influence the nature of your responses, of course. However, going through this thinking process periodically is a healthy exercise for any professional or business.

Once the mission statement is in a form that is reasonably satisfactory, many professionals find it valuable to have it reproduced and posted where it can be seen by those who are impacted by it. I have seen personal mission statements framed and posted as wall charts, laminated and put on a stand on the individual's desk, printed on the back of business cards, included in descriptive or promotional literature, added as a preamble to professional proposals, and presented in other imaginative ways. By keeping it visible and referring to it periodically, it becomes a living document which can increasingly influence your way of thinking and your planning decisions.

Exercise – Preparing Your Personal and Professional Mission Statement

This exercise needs to be included in your Strategic Planning Notebook. Review in detail the questions on the Appendix worksheet "Clarifying Your Personal and Professional Mission" to determine the extent to which they directly apply to you. Cross out any that clearly are not meaningful to you. Add any additional questions that you feel need looking into. Change any of the words or phrases in the questions to match the kinds of responses that you really need to have for your own mission statement. In other words, adapt the worksheet so that it will truly be useful to you.

Once you have determined the final set of questions you intend to use, duplicate the work sheet, insert it into your Notebook and distribute it to anyone else who will be involved in the process of developing your mission, including your facilitator. Then, isolate yourself somewhere where you will not be interrupted by telephones or people intruding and write down your own answers to these questions. If you come up against a mental block, you may wish to put the project aside and come back to it later. The physical act of actually writing something down is an important part of the decision-making process. It forces you to articulate thoughts that may be unclear in your mind.

After you have these questions answered so that you are reasonably comfortable with them, set aside some time to discuss them with with the other people who will be involved in the determination of your mission. You may find it desirable to get away to a neutral environment, possibly a vacation location, where you can concentrate completely on mission development. Then, with the assistance of your facilitator, review and assess your answers (and those of others who are involved). Complete candor among everyone participating is a very important condition for making this process work. When you have reached agreement on the answers to the questions, construct your own draft mission statement, using the examples as a model, and insert your answers and your draft statement into your Notebook.

In Summary

A statement of personal and professional mission provides the foundation from which all strategic and operational decisions should be made. It helps you:

- articulate the specific kind of business and profession in which you should be involved
- determine what *not* to do as you pursue your career and your life
- communicate your own philosophy and values, and
- create a professional image.

The basis for your mission statement can be determined by answering a series of penetrating questions designed to give you a broad picture of what needs to be addressed in your personal strategic plan. These should be answered by yourself and, possibly, with your spouse and/or others with a strong vested interest in how you pursue your profession. The development of your mission statement can be even more effective when you ask someone who does *not* have a strong vested interest to serve as a facilitator.

Once you have developed your mission statement to the point where you are reasonably satisfied with it, make it a living document that you refer to regularly as you approach the important decisions in your profession and your life. Your mission statement needs to be formally reviewed and modified (if appropriate) at least once a year or whenever you are faced with a significant change in the nature of your business, your career, or your life.

CHAPTER 5

Identifying Your Areas of Strategic Concern

HAVING ESTABLISHED your personal and professional mission, the next step is to begin to isolate those areas requiring significant attention because they affect your future plans. In this chapter, we will identify some of the areas that typically will cover your critical strategic issues.

For example, in the Financial area, if you happen to be planning to go into private practice, a critical strategic issue might be "need for sufficient cash reserves to underwrite start-up expenses and cover cash-flow requirements for the first two years of operation." Under Career Growth, "need for an advanced technical degree" could be a critical strategic issue, and in the Personal area there might be something like "ensuring sufficient quality time with the family."

This chapter is designed to give you an overview of areas that may affect your strategic planning. The following four chapters will go into considerably more detail. Use this chapter to highlight those areas that are of concern to you, then use the next four chapters selectively in exploring these areas in more detail and identifying and analyzing critical issues.

The Need for Focus

The principal reason for beginning to isolate areas of strategic concern is to establish a focus on where future efforts should be directed. Without this focus, there is a tendency to take a "shot gun" approach wherein we try to do a little bit of everything and nothing gets done very well. As you identify some of your potential areas of strategic concern, the process helps you to focus on the *six to eight most critical*, on which you need to concentrate your efforts. The fact that you may not have selected others as having critical strategic importance for you does not mean that some effort will not be devoted to them anyway.

The purpose in bringing focus on no more than six to eight is to make sure that you give conscious attention to the ones that will have the greatest future pay-off. For example, most professionals will give attention to new technological developments in their discipline regardless of whether or not it has been identified as a critical strategic issue. Therefore, unless you plan to play a significant role in creating the state-of-the-art in your profession, this probably will not be one of your strategic areas.

One concept that may help you focus on the issues is the Principle of the Vital Few (Figure 5.1). This is a graphic display of one of the principles of economics known as Pareto's Law or the 20-80 Principle. This suggests that you can divide all decisions or actions into three broad categories based on the cost of the input and the value of the output.

There are certain factors that have an input cost as low as 20 with an output value as high as 80. These are clearly the first category – "vital few." In business, 20% of your customers produce 80% of your business and 20% of your customers produce 80% of your customer-related problems. And they are not necessarily the same 20%. 20% of the projects you work on will produce 80% of the results of your efforts. The precise numbers are not important; the relationship, however, between input and output is very important to your decision making.

The second category, which has roughly an equal relationship between input and output, refers to the "routine" decisions we must make to maintain the status quo but where additional effort produces little in the way of additional results.

The final group, which is labeled the "trivial many," represents factors that frequently require an input cost of 80 to produce an output value of 20 or less.

While the "routine" and, to a certain extent, the "trivial many" may be addressed in your short term or operational planning, it is absolutely essential that your strategic planning efforts focus *exclusively* on the "vital few," those issues that will have a major impact on where you want to be in the future.

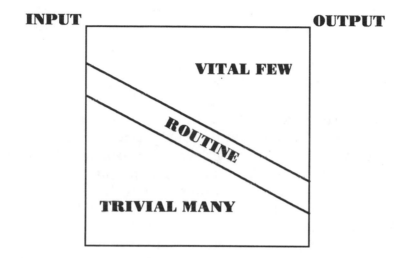

INPUT / OUTPUT / VITAL FEW / ROUTINE / TRIVIAL MANY

Figure 5.1: THE PRINCIPLE OF THE VITAL FEW

The Importance of Data

Valid and reliable data are the lifeblood of any strategic analysis effort. Data are needed to validate that the critical issue identified is in fact the *true* issue and not merely a perceived issue. For example, the need for an advanced degree in a particular technical discipline is only a perceived issue without sufficient data to evaluate it. In fact, it may turn out that there is already a glut of professionals with degrees in that discipline. Pursuing a more specialized type of training and experience, thereby establishing a niche for yourself that is not overcrowded, may prove to be a much more productive course of future action. As we get into more detail in later chapters, we will take a look at various ways in which such data can be acquired and how appropriate conclusions can be reached.

Determining Personal Preferences

One of the reasons many professionals are intrigued by the potential of going into private practice is that they believe this will enable them to do more of the things that have personal appeal to them than would be true if they remained in a larger organization. While this may be true to a certain extent, there is not nearly as wide a gap between being in private practice and working within an organization as many people would like to believe.

The fact that you may be in business for yourself rarely means that you have the license to do only those things that are personally satisfying. For example, many, if not most, professionals do not like to sell. Reality indicates, however, that as much as 50 to 75 % of your time and effort as an independent professional may have to be devoted to seeking out potential clients and turning them into revenue-producing customers, particularly at the outset of your business. Even a professional who is functioning in a mature business is likely to spend 25 to 30 % of his or her time and effort in sales. Contrast that with the fact that most professionals (other than those in sales) who operate within a larger organization will probably spend little, if any, time and effort in revenue-producing sales.

Clearly identifying personal preferences can have a major impact in shaping future professional efforts. If "freedom of choice" is of paramount importance, then the downside requirements will need to be examined as well. Determining what it is that you really *want* to do and what it is that you really *don't* want to do, professionally and personally, are essential factors in determining what will be the most productive and satisfying future direction for you.

Shopping List of Potential Areas

As a means of getting some focus on those strategic areas that you need to address in the future, let's first divide them into four broad categories: Personal, Career Growth, Business Development, and Financial. We will start with the Personal category, since that has more of a universal interest, and move on to the others in order, always remembering that the list is not exhaustive. Later in this chapter, you will find some simple decision-making techniques that will assist you in determining which have the highest priority for you. Then you will be in a position to select the six to eight most critical *areas* that you need to focus on in the future. Later chapters will help you identify critical *issues* and validate them for specific action.

● Personal

Family/Personal relationships include those people who may not be an active part of your profession or business but, nevertheless, represent an important part of your life. Unfortunately, for many professionals, this ends up being an area that does not get nearly the attention it deserves.

Health, rest and recreation includes whatever you might do to take care of your mind, body and spirit that, while it may not directly contribute to the pursuit of your profession, enables you to be more productive and fulfilled.

Cultural pursuits are specific activities that typically are not related to your profession. These could include such things as the arts, music, literature, hobbies, spiritual development, or anything that enhances your becoming a more fulfilled total person.

Service to church, community, profession speaks to a personal need that many professionals have. You need to determine how important it is for you to do something that will benefit others without any reward other than the personal satisfaction of having been of service.

Retirement, as I mentioned in Chapter 1, is frequently an emotion-laden issue for many professionals. Nevertheless, whether it is your intent to continue practicing your profession in some way once you have reached "retirement age," or to complete one phase of your life and then move on to another, at some point you probably will want to establish plans that can prepare you, financially and otherwise, for that time when your current professional activities will be neither possible nor desirable.

● Career Growth

Education could include such things as working toward advanced degrees, completion of particular courses of study, or anything whereby the completion of a set of specified requirements, typically requiring effort over several years, would be a significant contribution to your professional standing and/or marketability.

Certification/Licensing/Professional designations or recognition addresses the value and/or necessity of receiving an official "blessing" from a recognized body for the work that you do. These may or may not require additional education.

Research/Study usually involves professional effort (frequently reimbursed or underwritten by your employer or clients) that will lead to the achievement of results which will make a contribution to your profession or industry. These results may produce significant financial return, recognition, or an increase in your knowledge and capability.

Publications include books, articles, papers, research studies, software programs, video or audio cassettes, or anything where your efforts are recorded somewhere for the use of others. It is becoming increasingly evident in many professions that publication of one sort or another is an essential requirement in order to be considered in the upper echelons of that profession.

Affiliations represent such things as professional or trade associations, colleges or universities, business or community organizations, honor societies, professional networks, business consortiums, or any formal or informal organizations that can play a role in your professional education or skill development, your credibility or marketability, your need to contribute to your profession, or anything that enhances your image and satisfaction in the pursuit of your profession.

Work experience includes any employment, professional practice, or volunteer service that will contribute to your knowledge, skill and credibility within your profession. In many cases, it may prove desirable to accept a position with an organization for a limited period of time in order to gain experience, increase knowledge, or establish working relationships with certain people, all of which may have a significant impact on your future professional direction.

● Business Development

(The focus here will be almost entirely on professionals who are either in private practice or a part of a professional services firm.)

Services/Products incorporates all of those tangible and intangible revenue-producing things that you can offer to the market place currently or that you need to be prepared to offer some time in the future. These will be determined by your own knowledge and capability, the needs of your chosen market places, and future opportunities that may come along.

Clients/Customers/Markets gets you to identify those individuals and market segments (whether they are small or large businesses, governmental or non-profit organizations, as well as their geographical concentration and type of business), or customers (specific companies/organizations/individuals) with whom you already have an established business relationship or have access to. From a strategic planning point of view, this would also include identifying *potential* markets/customers that you wish to access at some point in the future, even though you may not be prepared to do so at the present time.

Marketing/Sales identifies your present and future *means* for accessing markets/customers. This could include, but is not limited to, such things as advertising/promotional efforts, sales methodology, use of outside marketing/sales services, image-building efforts, and referral systems.

Associates/Staffing will address such needs as support services (clerical, marketing/sales, research, etc.); professionals who may be full or part time employees; other principals with whom a current or future merger may seem desirable; and professional associates who operate independently but with whom some joint or sub-contracted efforts may be appropriate.

Business operations covers a myriad of things such as record keeping, billings and credit, preparation of support materials, correspondence, accounting/bookkeeping and legal considerations. This and sales are the two areas where many professionals tend to get bogged down. While you may be able to hire someone to take care of your business operations, you will still have to be involved in them, probably more than you would like.

● **Financial**

Cash flow, for most professionals, is probably the single most important financial concern, particularly at the outset. Ensuring that there is sufficient revenue coming in, whether that be salary, professional fees, residuals, retainers, or any of a variety of other sources, that is sufficient to at least meet your outgoing expenses (while, hopefully, providing a surplus in the form of profit or savings) is essential. This goes well beyond budgeting in that it forces you to assess ways of optimizing revenue opportunities and controlling expenses. For some people, this comes quite naturally while others may find this to be one of the most frustrating parts of future planning.

Capital requirements, including start-up costs for a new business, becomes a critical area for many professionals, particularly those in private practice. Your future planning must take into consideration both the kinds of capital investment you will need (facilities, equipment, franchise or licensing fees, outside services, etc.) and the potential sources for underwriting those expenses (savings, partnership fees, sale of stock, borrowed funds from banks, venture capital, friends or relatives, etc.).

Pricing and gross/net profit represents establishing the fees that need to be charged in order to bring in a sufficient amount of revenue over the cost of providing services. It probably will not surprise you that many professionals in private practice have little or no idea what it costs them to provide their services or what represents a fair return that justifies their continuing to provide such services.

Net worth represents your financial position assessed by determining the assets that you have, compared with the liabilities or obligations that you are facing.

Other specific areas in the Financial category could include cash reserves, investments, acquisitions/divestitures, vacations, purchasing or modifying a home, supporting children or other family members, or a wide variety of additional areas that may be of particular interest to you personally.

Exercise - Determining Your Areas of Strategic Concern

The problem, of course, is that in going through this extensive list of potential areas of strategic concern one might easily identify most, if not all, as needing serious attention. As I have stressed several times already, the key to effective strategic planning is establishing a *focus* on those areas that will have the greatest impact on your future. Figure 5.2 lists the potential areas we have covered in this chapter. (A copy of this, entitled "Selecting Your Areas of Strategic Concern," is also included in the Appendix.) There is space for you to include additional areas under each of the four headings in the event you have some that are not listed. Going through this exercise now may help you determine which will have a major impact on where you want to go with your profession and which portions of the next four chapters you wish to study more specifically. (You may want to duplicate this now and insert it into your Strategic Planning Notebook.)

Your first screening effort will be to go through the list and cross out any of the potential areas that: 1) have little or no impact on your own future direction, 2) are concerns that will probably be addressed routinely on an ongoing basis, or 3) represent urgent problem areas that need to be resolved within the next year (these should be dealt with in your operational plan and should not be allowed to cloud your strategic thinking).

Next, set some initial priorities on those areas that remain on your list. A quick technique for doing this is to label them A, B or C:

A = those areas where some significant changes *must* take place over the next several years

B = those areas that represent breakthrough factors for you but with which you have only limited experience, probably requiring some research and experimentation

C = those critical areas that are proceeding satisfactorily now but will require some review and modification to ensure your continued progress.

Figure 5.2: SELECTING YOUR AREAS OF STRATEGIC CONCERN

Potential Areas	Category A	B	C	Priority 1, 2, etc.	Selection	Notes
Personal						
Family/personal rel.						
Health, rest & recreation						
Cultural pursuits						
Service to others						
Retirement						
Career Growth						
Education						
Cert./lic./prof design.						
Research/study						
Publications						
Affiliations						
Work experience						
Business Development						
Services/products						
Clients/customers/mkts.						
Marketing/sales						
Associates/staffing						
Business operations						
Financial						
Cash flow						
Capital requirements						
Pricing, gross/net profit						
Net worth						

Then, for each of the A's you have identified, place them in numerical rank order in terms of their importance to the carrying out of your mission – priority #1 being most important, #2 next most, and so on. Do the same with those marked B and then C. In the Appendix, you will find a blank version of the Decision Matrix, described in Chapter 3, which may help you in this aspect of setting priorities.

Once you have separated the areas and placed them in some order of priority, you need to select not more than six to eight which will help determine your strategic focus. More than six to eight frequently leads to such dispersion of interest that few, if any, receive the attention they deserve. *You may even wish to concentrate on no more than three or four initially.* In all probability, you will have at least one strategic area in each of the four categories in order to ensure a balanced perspective in the future.

The fact that you did not select some of the areas does not mean that you will not be putting effort into them. It is just a matter of where you want to *focus* your more visible efforts. You may wish to review the other areas periodically to see if they need more attention than they are getting. This is one of the advantages in keeping this worksheet, and others with which you will be working, in your Strategic Planning Notebook – so you can refer to it regularly and take whatever actions may be required.

While many of your selected strategic areas will continue indefinitely as ones where you need to concentrate your efforts, some will change over time because they have been effectively addressed already, they have become less critical to your future, or, possibly, you are contemplating a shift in direction. Therefore, I recommend that you go through this prioritization exercise at least once a year or whenever you are faced with significant new opportunities or setbacks. As with your mission statement, there is a value in doing this each year as though your current list did not exist, in order to ensure the greatest amount of objectivity in your strategic planning efforts.

In Summary

The first step you need to address, after developing your personal and professional mission statement, is the identification of the six to eight most critical areas. Focusing on the "vital few" will enable you to give attention to those critical strategic issues that will affect your future. From that identification, you can determine how much additional data you will need to establish those areas that will have the greatest payoff. We have divided these into four broad categories: Personal, Career Growth, Business Development, and Financial. The next four chapters will go into each of these areas in considerably more detail.

CHAPTER 6

Strategic Analysis of Personal Areas

- ocarpenter-

THE MATERIAL ON STRATEGIC ANALYSIS which will be presented in the next four chapters needs to be used selectively. Unfortunately, we are familiar with the "paralysis by analysis" syndrome that affects many organizational planning efforts. This syndrome also may be present when you do your personal strategic planning. Therefore, my recommendation is that you read through *this* chapter to get an understanding of the analytic process we will be following. Then skim over the material in the following three chapters, making marginal notations related to those areas that are of particular concern to you.

The purpose of the ideas shared in these chapters is primarily to stimulate your thinking regarding issues you need to address as you develop your own strategic plan. Keeping your attention focussed on the "vital few" will increase the likelihood that your plan will get the attention it deserves.

While many of the areas covered in these chapters were identified in Chapter 5, they will be repeated and addressed in more detail here. Once again, I urge you to adapt, rather than adopt, the ideas presented here. Since we will be touching on some of these areas fairly lightly, you may wish to refer to the Bibliography for additional assistance.

As was discussed in earlier chapters, my feeling is that your personal plan must include consideration of many personal factors that are either unrelated or only indirectly related to the pursuit of your professional career and business. I believe very strongly that a balanced life must encompass things other than business and professional success. A natural temptation for many professionals is to adopt a "tunnel vision" approach to life. One of the values of the strategic planning process is that it can help you give appropriate attention to all important aspects of your life as you proceed with your plan.

Personal Areas to Consider

1. Family/Personal relationships are generally at the top of the list. The professional who has strong understanding and support at home is more likely to sustain effective on-the-job performance. While pursuit of a particular profession does require some personal sacrifices, particularly in the early stages of career development, experience has shown that allowing that sacrifice to become all-encompassing can be truly destructive. While your wife or husband does not necessarily have to be completely familiar with everything that goes on in your work life, it is unfair to exclude them completely from what constitutes the major part of your waking hours. Having someone who can share, even superficially, both the excitement and the frustration associated with the pursuit of your career and business objectives can and should be a very satisfying experience.

Also, one of the possible benefits of establishing a private practice is the opportunity to work in a collaborative relationship with your spouse. While there are many cautionary tales about the potential hazards of husband and wife both working and living together, my observation in my own life and in that of many of my colleagues, is that there are far more positive than negative consequences. My wife, Carol, and I have worked together in my professional practice since 1975. While we had outside offices at one time, we have been working out of our home for the past several years and have found it to be occasionally frustrating but mostly rewarding in an ongoing relationship. Whether or not this is an appropriate relationship for you and your spouse is something that you may wish to examine carefully and possibly include as one of your critical strategic issues.

It is also important to keep your children, parents and siblings aware of what is going on in your career progression. Children like to talk about what their parents do for a living and, conversely, parents generally like to discuss what their adult children are doing professionally. You are denying them a significant amount of gratification if you do not keep them reasonably well informed on what it is you do. In addition to updating them on your business and career progress, it is equally important for you to take a strong interest in those things in which they are involved and to spend some quality time together on matters unrelated to anyone's business or profession. The degree to which you demonstrate interest, understanding and affection toward other members of your family generally will have an equal and reciprocal reaction from them. Establishing a personal discipline to make your family relationships a win-win affair for all concerned may be one of the most important non-business activities in which you participate.

A balanced life would include a number of friends and acquaintances with entirely different occupations: neighbors, people from your place of worship, colleagues in service and community organizations, and people with whom you have developed personal relationships in a variety of ways over a period of time. These friends also wish to share in some of your excitement and frustrations but generally not to the same level as members of your family. In other words, don't become a complete bore in always talking about your own interests and concerns. Also, you will need to show the same kind of interest and support in their occupations as you would like them to give to you.

Unless you are reasonably well satisfied with the relationships you have established and maintained with your family and friends, it is probably an area that needs some attention as a critical issue.

2. Health, rest and recreation are things we can do to renew ourselves physically, mentally, spiritually and emotionally. While almost everyone talks about these factors in one way or another, they frequently do not give them the attention needed to make renewal a vital part of their lives. I am not referring primarily to substance abuse, although that is one that should receive serious attention if it is a problem for you. Rather, I am referring in broader terms to what you are doing, or not doing, to reinforce the human temple in which you reside. For example, how many professionals do you know (possibly even yourself) who seem to take a sense of pride and, possibly, martyrdom in the fact that they rarely, if ever, use all of their vacation time? One of the major purposes of a vacation, of course, is to provide a distinctly different kind of experience from normal work effort with a view toward giving us a fresh perspective and an opportunity for renewed energy in pursuing our primary profession.

Many professionals in private practice, in particular, get so involved in their business that they perceive they cannot take time off for activity that is not business related. This tends to be reinforced with the view, real or perceived, that such action will result in significant lost revenue. On the other hand, many other professionals in private practice view the freedom associated with owning their own business as an opportunity to place much more emphasis on rest and recreation.

For example, since the early 1980s, my wife and I have taken a minimum of one week's vacation every quarter. And, in several cases, we have been able to extend that to two or three weeks. Sometimes this is scheduled with a business trip, but frequently it is a stand-alone effort that goes on our calendar the same as if it were a business booking. Our plan, over the next few years, is to increase that to a minimum of four weeks of vacation per quarter. We find that this gives us not only an opportunity to spend time together where business is not the major focus but to examine and assess where we are going from both a business and personal perspective without the pressure of day to day business operations.

Unless the giving of sufficient time and attention to matters related to your health, rest and recreation are a built-in part of your personal discipline already, you should give strong consideration to establishing this as one of your critical strategic issues.

3. Cultural pursuits includes those activities that broaden our perspective and help us grow as human beings, without necessarily having a direct impact on our business or career plans. The primary benefit of these activities comes from personal satisfaction and growth. I am interpreting "culture" very broadly. It could include active or spectator participation in the arts, entertainment, sports, hobbies, educational or spiritual activities. Some professionals find it just as fulfilling, or even more so, to be recognized for their participation in activities such as community theater, musical groups, and amateur or professional sports as to be recognized in their primary professions.

As a means of strengthening and balancing your personal life, you may wish to consider focusing on the pursuit of certain cultural interests as one of your critical strategic issues.

4. Service to church, community, or profession represents a need that many people have – to give of themselves, where the only real benefit comes from the satisfaction of knowing that what you have done is of benefit to other people. Compensation, if any, is generally limited to expenses incurred. Such activities could range anywhere from assuming an elected or appointed leadership position, serving as a counselor or teacher in one of your areas of expertise, providing care and assistance to those who may be unable to satisfactorily provide it themselves (hospitals, rest homes, youth groups, etc.), to serving as a mentor for a newer member of your profession.

Service has been an important part of my adult life and has been an extremely fulfilling experience for me. I am very active in my church, having served in a number of leadership roles. I served for many years on our local YMCA Board of Directors, including a term as Chairman. I have been a contributing member of the Boards of Directors of two professional associations – the National Speaker's Association and the Association for Management Excellence (formerly the International MBO Institute), and have an ongoing mentoring relationship with some developing members of my profession. My service in these and other capacities has been an important enough value in my own life that I have turned down several opportunities for client business in order to fulfill my obligations.

Particularly, as we reach the more mature stages of our careers, the need to be of service to others frequently takes on an increasingly important role. If this is true for you, a critical strategic issue related to that would be an appropriate one to consider.

5. Retirement is a subject that many of us don't give serious attention to until it becomes critical, and then we are often without sufficient information. Planning for such things as a radical change in income as well as a different life style needs to become a part of our thinking by mid-career, if not earlier. This includes financial planning, where we intend to live, what we plan to do, and many other considerations that can be dealt with much more productively when we are not faced with a tremendous sense of urgency.

There are many excellent resources available to assist in planning for retirement (see your local library for a selection).

6. Others could include such things as strengthening your spiritual life, politics, pursuing an avocation or second career, home improvements, or anything else that represents worthwhile activity for you that is not directly related to the pursuit of your normal business or profession.

How to Complete a Personal Strategic Analysis

The purpose of the first portion of this chapter was to help you identify and isolate those personal issues that have critical strategic significance for your personal planning. Answering the following questions will help you move from issue to conclusion, thus enabling you to determine what your long term objectives and strategic action plans for these areas should be.

1. What is the critical strategic issue to be addressed? A critical issue, to be effectively dealt with, should be written out as a complete sentence. It represents a statement of concern that will have a major impact on your desired future which cannot be completely resolved in one year or less. For example, under Family Relationships, a critical issue might be "I need to devote considerably more time and attention to my aging parents over the next several years." Under Cultural Pursuits, you might have a critical issue like "I want to become much more knowledgeable on the subject of grand opera so I can enjoy it more." Under Service to my Profession, a mature professional could identify an issue such as "I want to pay back to my profession for the tremendous life I have had as a part of it."

At this stage, the accuracy of the issue statement is less critical than the identification of the subject matter. A validation process, as shown in the next step, will provide an opportunity for either modifying or significantly changing the way the issue is stated. By writing down one or more perceived critical issues, you will be in a better position to make an assessment as to the relative importance of each and whether or not you have captured their essence. If you should end up with several issues, you can then make a choice as to which ones are important enough to include in your plan.

2. What data do you have or need to validate this issue and to come up with effective ways of addressing it? If it represents a problem situation, what are the root causes? For example, in order to validate the issue related to Family Relationships, data could include a factual record of the frequency and nature of your visits to your parents in the past year, information related to their financial and physical health, and special interests they may have to which you could contribute. Some data you are seeking may be readily available while you may have to dig for others. The key is, before moving ahead with establishing plans to address a particular issue, you need to make certain that you are addressing the *right* issue.

3. What conclusions and/or alternative courses of action will effectively address the resolution of this issue? Now is the time to begin to place some focus on things that need to take place. For example, if the issue under Family Relationships, "I need to devote considerably more time and attention to my aging parents over the next several years," is still valid, appropriate conclusions might be:

a. I need to set aside specified times each week or month for quality time with my parents.
b. I need to plan vacations over the next few years in which my parents can participate.
c. I need to be more sensitive to their emotional, as well as physical, needs.

Alternative courses of action could identify various types of activity and/or vacations that might be appealing to the parents and which would be practical and desirable to pursue.

Examples of Data Analysis

Barbara Spangler, our PhD electronics engineer who is raising two children as a single parent, has determined a need to spend more quality time with her children. Mark Bellows, a systems analyst, wants to establish a plan for systematic health improvement. Jack Michaels, our accountant, has reached a point in his life where he wants to become more active in his church and community.

Figure 6.1: CRITICAL ISSUE ANALYSIS OF PERSONAL AREAS

Barbara Spangler, Electronics Engineer

Critical Issue

I need to spend more quality time with my children that does not detract from my on-the-job performance.

Supporting Data

● I have been divorced for three years. My former husband moved away from this area about six months ago. He is usually on time with his support payments. We remain on cordial terms.

- My daughter is ten and a good student who has difficulty making friends. My son is eight and an average student who is one of the most popular kids in his class. Both enjoy playing tennis. A neighbor watches them after school.

- My former husband spent considerable time with both children, particularly our son, while he was living in the area. Now he is able to see them only about three times a year — around holidays.

- My work schedule has been somewhat erratic because of the nature of some of the projects on which I have been working. My personal ambitions to advance have tended to reinforce this practice.

Conclusions

- I need to rearrange my work schedule so that I can plan my time for being with the children more predictably. (This can be done, but it requires some discipline on my part.)

- I need to work out a plan with the children for regularly scheduled activities, such as tennis, in which we can all participate, and for family time together when I can share with them what is happening in my working world and they can discuss with me what is happening at school and elsewhere. This also must include some one-on-one time with each of them.

- We need to jointly plan vacations that will be exciting, fulfilling and that we can all look forward to.

- I need to look ahead to when they will be teenagers and in high school and anticipate what changes in my relationship with them are both desirable and inevitable.

- I must also allow some quality time for myself, that is not directly related to either my work or my children, in order to maintain my sanity.

Mark Bellows, Systems Analyst

Critical Issue

I need to establish and implement a long range plan for health improvement and reinforcement.

Supporting Data

- I have made spasmodic attempts to get on an exercise program, but I inevitably get sidetracked.

- I am about 15 pounds over the desired weight for my size and age. I am in generally good health except for that.

- My job is sedentary with little opportunity for exercise during working hours.

Conclusions

- I need to establish a health improvement plan with some built-in incentives for continuing and expanding it.

- Alternatives to consider:
  - Annual physical (my company will cover cost)
  - Join a health club (required payments should increase my incentive to continue)
  - Establish a joint exercise plan with my wife
  - Establish a joint exercise plan with one or more friends or business colleagues
  - Establish increasingly challenging targets for physical achievement, rewarding myself when I achieve specified milestones
  - Establish a nutrition plan with assistance from my doctor or a nutritionist
  - Establish and maintain a progress chart that can remind me daily of my commitment
  - Make a written commitment to my wife and ask her to be my disciplinarian

- Review and modify my plan every six months in line with my current status and projected goals

---

Jack Michaels, Accountant

Critical Issue

I want to use my skills as a means of service to my church and community.

Supporting Data

- I have turned down requests in the past to provide such assistance on the grounds that "I'm too busy." I'm not.

- I have a strong interest in my church and also the YMCA in my community (having been an active member in my youth). I am limited in what I can give financially, but I can support them through service, using my accounting and organizational skills.

Conclusions

- I want to commit a certain number of hours per month to service to my church and to the YMCA, starting modestly and taking on additional responsibilities as I become comfortable in my role.

- Alternatives to consider:
  - Auditing
  - Serving as Treasurer or in another volunteer financial position
  - Serving on a task force to design and/or modify accounting/reporting systems
  - Serving on a Finance Committee
  - Serving on a Board
  - Teaching basic accounting to staff, members and/or volunteers
  - Assisting with fund raising

Exercise – Developing Your Personal Analysis

You may wish to insert several copies of the worksheet entitled "Critical Issue Analysis of Personal Areas" (in the Appendix) into your Strategic Planning Notebook. Then select the particular issues that you want to focus on now and complete your analysis. As you get comfortable in this approach to strategic analysis, you may find ways to speed up the process. But, resist the temptation to jump immediately into solutions before you have validated the issue.

In Summary

Strategic analysis in personal areas is the first of the four major categories we are focussing on in this section. It is the one that we tend to overlook the most, yet is the one that is essential to achieving a balanced life. I have identified four primary areas within this category: family/personal relationships, health, rest and recreation, cultural pursuits, and service to church, community or profession. You may have identified others that are even more meaningful to you. The important thing to remember is that your life is only partially fulfilled if you don't look seriously, and strategically, at those areas that are not directly related to your business and your profession.

CHAPTER 7

Strategic Analysis Of Career Growth Areas

-©carpenter92-

CAREER GROWTH CAN BE DEFINED as anything that will increase your competence and/or credibility in your chosen profession. This definition is equally applicable if you are considering changing or modifying your profession. We recognize, of course, that professional growth is a journey and not a destination. Presumably, any serious professional operates in a continuing quest for increased competence and credibility. For strategic planning purposes, however, I will concentrate on those areas where significant achievements or milestones are critical to future positioning in your profession or business.

Career Growth Areas to Consider

1. Education refers both to the completion of educational requirements for college or university degrees and to the undertaking of specific courses of study. There is no doubt that, in many professions, the granting of one or more accredited degrees will significantly enhance the credibility (and presumably the competence) and marketability of the individual who achieves it. This is especially true for individuals who are seeking their first professional position. Having an undergraduate or advanced degree from a reputable institution of learning will certainly make the search for an initial position within an organization easier to attain.

In certain professions, particularly those of a technical nature, the regular pursuit of advanced degrees is both encouraged and rewarded. Ironically, however, once you have been in the field for a period of time, advanced degrees generally carry considerably less impact than your experience and accomplishments (unless you intend to continue a career in academia). For example, in my career as a speaker/trainer/consultant, the only times I have ever been asked about my educational background is when my efforts have been associated with a university or it has been a matter of curiosity with a particular individual within a client organization. While I have both BS and MEd degrees, they have very little relevance to the work in which I am involved today. As a matter of fact, because I have authored several books, many people assume I have a doctorate and address me as such, something I was embarrassed by earlier in my career but have fun with today.

With the major emphasis that is placed on grade point average in most educational institutions, it is ironic that about the only time it is given consideration is during the initial screening process for the first after-college position, and I'm not sure that it is even of significant importance then.

One word of caution: beware of degrees granted by "diploma mills" and other non-accredited institutions. Even if a significant amount of effort is put into achieving such a degree, a wide perception by employers and clients alike is that there is something phony about it, which is likely to reduce the legitimate credibility you have built up.

2. Certification/Licensing/Professional designation or recognition, in many professions, carries more weight than a college or university degree. Even though an accredited degree may be a requirement for lawyers, dentists or physicians, for example, they cannot practice their professions without having passed the state bar examination or been licensed by the official state professional association or society. Almost every accepted profession has one or more forms of certifying or recognizing members who have reached certain milestones.

These may include formal education, continuing education, specific work experience, affiliation with professional organizations, length of time in practice, and client verification.

Following are some of the more recognizable forms of certification or recognition: CPA (Certified Public Accountant), PA (Public Accountant), PE (Professional Engineer), RN (Registered Nurse), LVN (Licensed Vocational Nurse), CLU (Chartered Life Underwriter), CAE (Certified Association Executive), CMP (Certified Meeting Professional), CSP (Certified Speaking Professional), CMC (Certified Management Consultant), and many, many more. You will want to become familiar, if you are not already, with all of the certifications, licenses, professional designations or recognitions that have value in your chosen profession.

3. Research/Study, particularly in technical or scientific professions, may be an especially important vehicle for establishing your competence and/or credibility. Clearly, being able to demonstrate scientifically-proven contributions to the state-of-the-art in your profession may be the most powerful way for you to set yourself apart from your professional colleagues. However, you must recognize that this type of research or study is generally quite expensive in terms of both time and other resources. Therefore, most such research or study effort will take place within a college or university or in an organization where it is both encouraged and funded. It is a rare professional in private practice who can afford to pursue such effort on an extended basis.

4. Publication represents an excellent way in almost any profession to achieve recognition and enhanced credibility. This can include, but is not limited to, such things as books, anthologies, professional journal and magazine articles, professional papers delivered at symposia, audio or video tapes, monographs or pamphlets, and software. The many books and other publications which I have authored or coauthored represent by far the most important vehicle I have had both for establishing my professional credibility and for marketing purposes.

While publication can also represent a significant source of income, the primary value to most professionals lies in the credibility that it creates. One technique that I have used quite effectively is to take portions of a book that I have recently written, or am in the process of writing, and publish them in recognized journals or magazines or for self-distribution. Other authors have found it effective to start with a series of articles, eventually converting them into a book. There are many resources available (see Bibliography) that can help you pursue the publication route, if that is your desire.

A word of caution here: make certain that whatever you publish and have distributed clearly presents you and your ideas positively and positions you correctly. Having something published prematurely could have a boomerang effect on your career; an axiom that is quoted frequently at the National Speakers Association is that "you get better over time, but the books and tapes you have already published do not."

5. Affiliations with professional organizations and other groups may be an important means for strengthening your professional position. Here you can meet regularly with other professionals and/or potential clients or employers. My affiliations with the National Speakers Association, the American Society for Training and Development, and the Association for Management Excellence (formerly the International MBO Institute) have been tremendously valuable for professional networking, sources of knowledge and skill development, and avenues of professional recognition and visibility.

There is a truism related to affiliations that "you get from it in direct proportion to that which you give to it." Joining an organization strictly for the purpose of being able to say that you are a member carries little value. The most successful professionals, frequently, are ones who have been active in their professional organizations through regular attendance, program leadership and participation, mentoring other professionals, and board/committee/task force participation. For some professionals, affiliations may represent more of an ongoing operational consideration while, for others, it may be vitally important from a strategic perspective.

6. Work experience, in the long run, is likely to serve as one of the most, if not *the most,* important vehicles for both improving your professional competence and enhancing your credibility. Particularly in the early stages of your career, a major consideration in accepting a position within an organization should be how the work experience you will have will position you more effectively for the future. This is true whether you see your future within an organization, as part of a professional services firm, or in private practice.

As mentioned earlier in this book, I have made two major career changes during my life: first, moving from that of a YMCA professional into the field of management training and development within industry and government; second, moving into my current career as a full time speaker/trainer/consultant. My first career change was more a matter of happenstance which, fortunately, took me in a career direction which was highly appropriate for me. My second career change came about with much more foresight and planning. After determining that private practice was my future, each of the two job shifts I made were selected with a view to gaining knowledge and experience that would enhance my credibility when I finally decided to go out on my own. Clearly your accomplishments and work experience will be major factors when being considered for promotion within an organization or for recruitment to another. The more relevant your experience is to the position for which you are being considered, the greater likelihood there will be for a favorable decision.

In the early stages of private practice, one of the biggest hurdles that professionals have to overcome is the question asked by prospective clients about who you have worked with previously and what, specifically, you have done with and for them. This reinforces the need for having adequate cash reserves when starting in private practice so that you can afford to be somewhat selective in the kinds of clients with whom you initially work. As you proceed further in the advancement of your career, whether within an organization or on your own, you may wish to focus your efforts in such a way that you will be perceived as a specialist in what you do.

7. Others, while probably having more of an operational flavor, could include developmental efforts such as professional reading, seminar/conference/symposia participation, informal networking groups, or anything else that could contribute to improving your professional competence and/or enhancing your credibility.

How to Complete a Career Growth Analysis

Chapter 6 described the approach, so I will concentrate here on relevant examples.

1. What is the critical strategic issue to be addressed?

Strategic Area	Critical Issue
Education	An advanced degree is a requirement for me to be considered for advancement to the next higher classification.
Publication	Publication in recognized journals of my profession is necessary to set me apart from other professionals with whom I might be competing.
Work experience	At least two years' experience in a line, rather than a staff, position will significantly improve my credibility with potential clients when I move into private practice.

2. What data do you have or need to validate this issue and to come up with effective ways of addressing it? If it represents a problem situation, what are the root causes?

For example, in order to validate the issue related to Education, data could include a stated company policy of qualifications for promotion, or you might check the records of recent promotions to the classification you are seeking that would support your position. It might also prove useful to identify what specific degrees or disciplines tend to be viewed favorably. Also, your data may suggest that the completion of a certificated course of study, which could be completed in a shorter period of time, may be just as acceptable as an advanced degree for promotion consideration.

3. What conclusions and/or alternative courses of action will effectively address the resolution of this issue?

For example, if the issue originally identified under Education "An advanced degree is a requirement for me to be considered for advancement to the next higher classification" is still valid, appropriate conclusions might be:

> a. I need to make a commitment of the time and money required to get the degree.
>
> b. I need to enlist the support of my supervisor and other relevant company officials.
>
> c. I need to determine what specific degree and/or discipline is best for me.

Alternative courses of action related to the commitment of time and money could include a concentrated program requiring a reduced workload or, possibly, a leave of absence, or a longer program that could be completed on evenings and weekends without unduly affecting work schedules.

Examples of Data Analysis

Shirley Jasper, our first example, is a Buyer in the Purchasing Department of a medium sized growth oriented manufacturing company. She has a BS degree in Electrical Engineering, but moved into Purchasing with a previous employer when she found the engineering work unfulfilling. She has set her sights on becoming a Purchasing Manager and has identified what she needs to accomplish to position herself for such opportunities.

Our second example is Andy Lampson, an architect in a regional office of a major architectural firm. He would like to become a principal or partner in an established architectural firm and has determined that, if he is to realize that goal, he must prepare for and receive his professional registration from AIA (American Institute of Architects) as well as work in progressively more responsible positions, possibly in different locations.

Charles Anderson, a marketing consultant with a strong marketing background who has been in private practice for three years, is our third example. He recognizes the need for establishing credibility that sets him apart from the competition and has determined that publishing is the route he will follow. He is examining several alternatives.

Figure 7.1: CRITICAL ISSUE ANALYSIS OF CAREER GROWTH AREAS

Shirley Jasper, Buyer in a Growth-Oriented Manufacturing Company. Married, 32 years of age, two children in grade school

---

Critical Issue

An advanced degree and more diversified experience are needed for me to achieve my career goal of Purchasing Manager in this or another company.

Supporting Data

- The current Purchasing Manager is expected to retire in about six years.

- This company places a high value on advanced degrees. The current Purchasing Manager has an MBA.

- I have a BS in Electrical Engineering, completed eight years ago.

- My role in Purchasing for the past four years has been as a Buyer for the Electrical Systems Division.

- The company has three other divisions with different technical disciplines.

Root Causes

- I started out as an electrical engineer in another company following graduation from college and discovered I did not enjoy that. I moved into Purchasing as an Assistant Buyer with that company three years later and discovered my niche. I was hired by my present employer as a Buyer two years after that because of my degree and my Purchasing experience.

- My family responsibilities until now have prevented me from pursuing an advanced degree.

- I have stayed in my role as Buyer for the Electrical Systems Division because of my comfort level there and my employer's perception that my expertise can be best utilized there.

Conclusions

- I must begin work on my MBA next semester.

- I need to reach agreement with my husband and children on my need for an advanced degree and for their support while I am working on it.

- I need to establish a mentoring/career counseling relationship with the current Purchasing Manager or someone else who can guide me.

- I need to gain a working knowledge of and experience in each of the other divisions within the company.

Andy Lampson, Architect in a Regional Office for a Major Architectural Firm. Single, 27 years of age

---

Critical Issue

I need to prepare for and receive my professional registration from AIA and be placed in progressively more responsible positions in order to reach my goal of becoming a principal or partner in an established architectural firm.

Supporting Data

- All active partners in this firm have their professional registrations and have held several positions at different locations within the firm. Similar patterns exist in most other major firms.

- In my four years with this firm, I have been successful with increasingly challenging assignments although my status within the firm has not changed as yet.

- I have been told by senior members of this firm that my record to date indicates that I have the potential to become a partner.

Conclusions

- I need to complete the requirements and apply for professional registration.

- I need to establish, in cooperation with a senior member of the firm, a career path that will include advancement to progressively more responsible positions, including geographical relocations as appropriate.

Charles Anderson, Marketing Consultant in Private Practice (three years). Married, 38 years of age, three children

---

Critical Issue

I need to be a published author in order to establish the credibility necessary to move me to the next higher level in my field.

Supporting Data

- My experience as a marketing manager in two different industries and my three years as a marketing consultant provide me with a good experiential background and puts me in a fair competitive position with other marketing consultants.

- I need something to set me apart from other consultants; becoming a published author is an effective way to get that special credibility.

- My approach to "spontaneous marketing" has some distinct differences that lends itself to publication. There are no other publications that I am aware of that promote this specific approach.

Conclusions

- I need to establish a plan leading to multiple publications within the next two to three years.

- Alternatives to consider:
  - Book published by a well-known publisher
  - Book published by a smaller, lesser-known publisher
  - Self-published book
  - Articles published in well-known sales and marketing magazines
  - Articles published in business journals
  - Articles published in trade association magazines
  - Pamphlets or monographs published on the subject
  - Chapter in an anthology
  - Newsletter, mine or others

- Alternative ways of accessing publication outlets
  - Retaining an agent to secure a publishing contract
  - Sending query letters to selected publishers
  - Networking with colleagues who are published
  - Attending American Booksellers Convention and/or other trade shows where publishers are exhibiting and discussing potential with publishers' representatives
  - Reviewing selected magazines and journals and sending query letters to those that appear to publish compatible articles
  - Subscribing to selected Writers Guild publications
  - Retaining a consultant who specializes in self-publishing

Exercise – Developing Your Career Growth Analysis

As recommended in Chapter 6, I suggest that you start by making several copies of the worksheet, "Critical Issue Analysis of Career Growth Areas," (in the Appendix) and inserting them into your Strategic Planning Notebook. Then, identify no more than three issues in the career growth area that are critical to your future positioning. Once again, reviewing Figure 5.2, "Selecting Your Areas of Strategic Concern," on page 78 may help get you started. Write down each issue you intend to work on as specifically as possible, on a separate worksheet. Then proceed with the analysis as illustrated in the explanations and examples in this chapter, identifying any additional data you may need. Don't forget the value of getting someone else involved in this analysis. Once you have completed your analysis of each of these issues, you will be in a position to make more effective choices on where you need to go from here.

In Summary

Career growth has to be one of the most important strategic areas for the career-minded professional. Even those professionals who may have reached the ultimate point in their careers find it both important and desirable to keep growing in order to feel fulfilled in what they are doing. Typically, career growth issues will fall under the following categories: education, certification/licensing/professional designation or recognition, research/study, publications, affiliations, and work experience, although this is not an exhaustive list. Focusing on the *right* issues that will have the greatest impact on your future is what strategic analysis is all about.

CHAPTER 8

Strategic Analysis of Business Development Areas

WHILE THE FOCUS in this chapter will be primarily on those professionals who are either in private practice or working within a professional services firm, some of the ideas could be helpful if you are employed within a larger organization, for two reasons: on the one hand they may be useful in determining how to position the *organization's* business; on the other, as a vehicle for marketing your own talents.

As with the prior two chapters, I recommend that you skim this chapter to get a general flavor of its approach and then apply the ideas on a selective basis, choosing those portions that are especially important to your strategic positioning. (Please note: I have included several worksheets for analyzing various aspects of a business. These will be useful *only* if new product/service development or marketing/sales are major concerns to you. If they are not major concerns, I suggest you skip over the explanations related to these worksheets.)

Business Development Areas to Consider

1. Services/Products represent those tangible "client deliverables" (the results of your work) which constitute the primary thrust of your business and which generate its revenue. While some of these primary services and products will be fairly obvious, others less obvious may have significant potential that may help position you more effectively for the kind of business in which you will be involved in the future.

One technique that may prove helpful in this area is illustrated in Figure 8.1 (Current Service/Product Assessment), as applied to my business in 1990. (A blank version of this worksheet is included in the Appendix for your own use.) Your first step would be to list all the services and products that you are currently capable of delivering. Then, following the designations at the top of the matrix in Figure 8.1, make your assessment regarding each of these factors for each of the services and products you have identified. You can make a simple assessment using something like High, Medium and Low or use a scale of one (low) to five (high) for each of the line items.

The first vertical factor I have labeled **Capability**. Here you would assess how well you are prepared to offer that kind of service or product to the marketplace. A High or 5 rating indicates that you are as well or better prepared to offer that item as any other practicing professional. A lower rating would suggest that you either need to do something to increase your capability or be prepared to offer a lower quality version perhaps at a lower cost. It is important at this stage to be completely honest with yourself as you make this type of an assessment. You may find it useful to have someone else go through this exercise with you to reduce the possibility of your being either too optimistic or too pessimistic.

The second factor, **Demand**, asks you to make an assessment of what you see as the potential for that particular service or product in the marketplace. This may be based on pure gut feeling or you may wish to do some sort of market-needs analysis. A high rating in this column would certainly indicate that this is something worth putting significant effort into. A low or medium rating, on the other hand, would suggest either that this item be given a lower priority or that significant effort may need to be invested in creating a perceived need on the part of potential clients.

Competition, the third factor, asks you to make a judge-

Figure 8.1: CURRENT SERVICE/PRODUCT ASSESSMENT
George Morrisey (1990)

SERVICES/PRODUCTS	CAPABILITY	DEMAND	COMPETITION	FEE/PRICE	COST	DESIRE
Speaking						
● Creating Your Future	5	3	3	3	2	5
● Strategic Planning	5	3	2	3	2	5
● Operational Planning	5	2	2	3	2	5
● Goal Setting	5	4	4	3	2	5
Training						
● Strategic Planning	5	3	2	3	2	4
● Operational Planning	5	3	2	3	2	4
● Management By Objectives	5	2	2	3	2	3
● Practical Self-Management	5	3	2	3	2	3
● Goal Setting	5	3	4	3	2	3
● Performance Appraisal	5	2	3	3	2	2
● Effective Presentations	4	3	4	3	3	1
Consulting/Facilitating						
● Strategic Planning	5	4	4	3	3	5
● Operational Planning	5	2	3	3	3	5
● Management By Objectives	5	2	3	3	3	3
● Performance Appraisal	5	2	4	3	3	3
Publications						
● Strategic Planning						
• Book	5	4	4	2	0	5
● Operational Planning						
• Book	5	3	2	2	0	5
● Management By Objectives						
• Business Book	5	2	2	2	0	4
• Public Sector Book	5	2	2	2	0	4
• Audio Program	5	2	2	3	2	4
• Video Program	3	1	2	3	2	2
● Performance Appraisal						
• Business Book	5	1	2	2	0	3
• Public Sector Book	5	1	2	2	0	3
● Goal Setting						
• Book	5	2	4	1	0	3
• Audio	5	2	4	3	2	3
● Effective Presentations	5	5	3	2	0	3

ment related to how many other firms or individuals are prepared to offer a similar service or product to the marketplace. A
high rating, indicating significant competition, does not necessarily mean that you should avoid this particular service or
product but it does suggest that your marketing efforts will
have to keep the competition in mind. On the other hand, if
there is relatively little competition in that particular service or
product, you may have a potential gold mine, provided there is
a high perceived need on the part of clients.

Fee/Price asks you to assess the level of revenue you can
anticipate receiving from the provision of such a service or
product.

Cost, on the other hand, asks you to make a similar assessment in terms of the actual cost of delivering that service or
product, including the amount of time you would have to
invest in it. Comparing these last two factors should help you
determine the profit potential you might find from offering that
particular service or product.

Desire asks you to assess how much you really want to do
what is required to provide that particular service or product.
A professional has to be a bit masochistic to offer a service or
product that he or she really dislikes providing, even if there is
a high profit potential. On the other hand, a strong desire to
provide a particular service or product could help offset negative factors. (Blank columns are included in the appendix
version so you can insert any other factors that may be worthwhile evaluating.)

The purpose of this particular tool is to provide you with a
broader base of insight as you make a determination of which
services or products to offer.

Figure 8.2, again shown as applied to my business (with a
blank version in the Appendix) asks you to identify some
potential services or products that could be a worthwhile addition to your business portfolio at some time in the *future*. I
suggest that you be a bit free-thinking in using this tool, allowing yourself to list services and products that are nothing more
than a "good idea" at the moment. The assessment process
would be essentially the same as in Figure 8.1 except that I have

Figure 8.2: FUTURE SERVICE/PRODUCT ASSESSMENT
George Morrisey (1990)

SERVICES/PRODUCTS	CAPABILITY	DEMAND	COMPETITION	FEE/PRICE	COST	DESIRE	PREPARATION	TIMING
Speaking								
● Creating Your Future								
• Customized	5	3	2	4	2	5	3	1+
● Developing Your Future	5	3	2	3	2	5	2	3
• Customized	5	3	2	4	2	5	3	3
Training								
● Creating Your Future	5	2	2	4	2	3	3	1+
● Developing Your Future	5	2	2	4	2	3	3	3
Publications								
● Creating Your Future								
• Generic Book	5	4	2	2	0	5	3	2
• Targeted Books	5	3	1	3	2	5	2	3+
• Audio	5	3	2	3	2	5	2	2
• Video	5	2	2	4	3	5	2	2+
● Developing Your Future								
• Generic Book	5	3	2	2	0	4	3	3+
• Targeted Books	5	3	1	3	2	4	2	4+
• Audio	5	3	2	3	2	4	2	4+
• Video	5	2	2	4	3	4	3	4+
● Strategic Planning								
• Audio	5	3	2	3	2	4	2	2
• Video	5	2	2	4	3	4	2	2
● Operational Planning								
• Audio	5	2	1	3	2	3	2	2
• Video	5	2	1	4	3	3	2	2
● Additional Business Books	5	3	3	2	2	5	3	4+
● Fictional Books	3	?	5	?	?	5	4	4+

added two additional columns: **Preparation** in which you would assess how much effort would be required to have that service or product available, and **Timing** where you would insert a number representing how many years in the future you think it might be appropriate and practical to introduce it.

These assessment tools should be used at least once a year

and at any other time during the year when a new service or product idea is identified, or an existing one does not appear to be living up to your expectations. Going through this analysis has helped me determine, on an ongoing basis, which services and products need to be phased out and which ones should be developed because they have the greatest potential for the future.

2. Clients/Customers/Markets represent those individuals and market segments (by industry, profession, geographical location, etc.) that either are now, or could be, users of your services and products. Whether you prefer to use the term "client" or "customer" is a matter of personal choice, the reference is to specific *individuals*, not organizations. If the services you offer them are primarily of a personal nature, such as income tax preparation, psychological counseling, or dentistry, you may find it useful to use the worksheet in Figure 8.3 to develop a profile of the type of individual you wish to serve.

If your services, such as engineering, business accounting, or consulting and training, are appropriate to organizations, then Figure 8.4 will help you focus on the kinds of organizations that have the greatest potential as well as identify who the decision makers and influencers might be.

Figure 8.3 is an illustration of how this worksheet was completed by Paula Dietrich, a financial planner. This provided her with a means of targeting the types of individual clients she wants to work with.

Figure 8.4 is another example drawn from my own consulting business which has helped me put my marketing and sales efforts in the right areas. (Blank versions of both worksheets are in the Appendix.)

There are many publications available that can provide you with substantial help in client/customer/market analysis. Therefore, I have been deliberately brief and superficial in its treatment. For many professionals, this particular area is a much more critical consideration than the one related to services/ products. If this is a major concern for you, then you would be well advised to establish this as one of your critical strategic issues.

Figure 8.3: CHECKLIST FOR DETERMINING
YOUR PREFERRED INDIVIDUAL CLIENT/CUSTOMER PROFILE

Paula Dietrich, Financial Planner

AGE RANGE: ___Infants/preschool ___ Preteens ___Teens
___20-35*√_ 36-50*√_50-65 _____ Retirees ___ Aged
Comments:

GENDER/MARITAL STATUS: ___ Female ___Male _*√_ Either
_*√_Couples ___ Married ___Single ___Divorced/Separated
___Widowed
Comments: Marital status not important

OCCUPATIONS: *√ Business Owners *√ Professionals *√ Managers
*√ Executives *√ Sales *√ Technical √ Blue Collar___Students
___Unemployed
___Others (Specify) _____

Comments:

ANNUAL INCOME: ___$0-10,000 ___$10,000-25,000_√ $25,000-50,000
*√ $50,000-100,000 *√ $100,000-500,000 √ $500,000+

Comments: Need to have discretionary income and cash
reserves

GEOGRAPHICAL AREA: *√ Local *√ Commuting Distance √ In-State
___In-Region ___National ___North America ___Worldwide
___Other (Specify)_____
Comments:

METHOD OF PAYMENT:* √ Cash √ Credit Card √ Open Account
___Installment *√ Retainer √ Company Charge ___Insurance
___Other (Specify) _____

Comments:

OTHER CONSIDERATIONS:

Prefer clients who have not previously used financial
planning services

* = Preferred Choices

---

3. Marketing/Sales, whether we like it or not, is an essential part of any business operation, including that of professional services. It is even essential for the professional who is now, and expects to remain, a part of a larger organization because of the continuing need to sell ideas and services, internally as well as externally. Periodically, I receive calls from experienced professionals employed within organizations who are contemplating entering the field of consulting. One of the initial questions I always ask is, "How do you feel about selling?" The answer frequently is, "I don't want to sell, I want to consult." My response then is, "With whom?" Regardless of how good you may be at what you do and how much need there is in the marketplace for such a service, clients do not normally come looking for people who can provide them with professional services. You must go to them.

Whether you intend to rely on personal referrals, advertising, direct mail, the telephone, a referral service, or some other vehicle, you need to have a clear plan in mind as to how you intend to reach the people you would like to serve. Once again, there are many publications and other forms of assistance that can help you develop a marketing/sales plan. Therefore, it is not my intent to do any more than identify this as a potential strategic area.

4. Associates/Staffing. While the vast majority of professionals who go into private practice end up as solo practitioners, there are two areas where it may be desirable or even necessary to formally or informally involve others.

The first is when there is a need for associates in the same profession who can complement or supplement your services from time to time. At one time, fairly early in my career as a full time consultant, there were three other consultants who were minority partners within my company. After a relatively short period of time in operating this way, I reached the conclusion that such an arrangement was not profitable and that it forced me to engage more heavily in certain activities, such as marketing and sales, than I had intended when I got into the business in the first place. Gradually, I reached an agreement with each of the other people to separate the formal relationship in favor

---

Figure 8.4: CHECKLIST FOR DETERMINING YOUR PREFERRED ORGANIZATIONAL CLIENT/CUSTOMER PROFILE

George Morrisey, Planning Process Consultant

TYPE OF BUSINESS: _* √ Manufacturer_* √ Retail_* √ Wholesale_
* √ Distributor_* √ Service_* √ Government_* √ Not-for-Profit
___Other (Specify)_____

Comments: Our process is generic and can be adapted to any type of business. I have worked with organizations in each of the above areas.

SIZE (NUMBER OF EMPLOYEES): _√ 1-10 √ 11-50 *√ 51-100 *√ 101-500
*√ 501-1,000 *√ 1,000-5,000 *√ 5,000-10,000 √ 10,000+_

Comments: Our process is applicable to any size organization; however, many smaller companies cannot afford our services and many larger companies perceive that they have an internal capability that can do what I do.

TYPE OF ORGANIZATION: _√ Proprietorship *√ Partnership
*√ Corporation *√ Family Owned *√ Single Location *√ Multiple Locations
____Other (Specify) _____

Comments: Many proprietorships would not be large enough to justify my services.

GEOGRAPHICAL CONSIDERATIONS: *√ Local *√ Commuting Distance
*√ In-State *√ In-Region *√ National *√ North America √ Worldwide
____Other (Specify) _____

Comments: I enjoy working in a variety of locations. Worldwide clients tend to be more interested in speaking, training or initial consulting assignments only because of the problems with distance in providing follow-up services.

SPECIAL CHARACTERISTICS: *√ Fast Growth *√ High Tech *√ Low Tech
*√ Centralized *√ Decentralized √ Franchise √ Turnaround
____Other (Specify) _____

Comments: Our process can apply in any type of organization. I have less experience working in Franchise or Turnaround situations.

DECISION MAKERS/INFLUENCERS : (Mark *M* if principal Decision Maker; *I* if Decision Influencer):_M_ CEO/COO _I_ Finance/Administration _I_ Human Resources ____Production ____Purchasing ____Sales ____Other (Specify) _____

Comments: Most of my entries into organizations come from the first three categories with CEO or COO approval necessary.

* = Preferred Choices

---

of one of a more informal nature. My practice today is as a solo practitioner with an informal network of other professionals I can call on whenever there is a need for additional professional assistance.

If the nature of your business is such that a formal partnership with other professionals is appropriate, then careful thought and planning must be invested in how that relationship should be established and maintained. Unfortunately, there are many horror stories about professionals, who have been good friends and colleagues, joining in a business venture only to have a period of disillusionment and even business failure as a result. Be extremely careful in the way you structure such a relationship, if that is a direction you wish to go, recognizing that it is usually a lot easier to form such a relationship than it is to dissolve it.

Staffing, the second area for involving others, usually refers to those people you wish to retain to perform services vital to your business operations that you choose not to perform yourself because it is not economical, you are not competent, or you simply prefer not to. This could include clerical and other support operations and para-professional services such as research, marketing and sales. Initially, in a start-up operation, you may wish to contract with an outside organization, such as a secretarial service, or hire a part-time employee (there are many very competent people who are interested in part time employment) until your practice is established sufficiently to justify a full-time working relationship. In many ways, particularly with a very small practice, compatibility of personalities is more important than technical ability of the individual being considered.

5. Business operations include all those aspects of your practice other than the actual delivery of revenue-producing services and products. These include such things as office and/or operating facilities, business equipment and supplies, telephone and other utilities, accounting, clerical and record-keeping services. Many an otherwise highly competent professional has been less successful than he or she could have been because of lack of adequate consideration to these other aspects of the business.

The key word there is *business*. While it may be obvious, it is important to keep continually in mind that a private professional practice is, in fact, a business, not a hobby. Some of the aspects of business operations can be addressed through staffing as suggested in item 4 above (though this will not relieve you of the real responsibility, as a principal in the firm, to stay on top of what is happening in business operations).

While many things related to business operations will be more of an operational or short term nature, you may wish to consider this as a critical strategic issue if you see your business significantly expanding or moving in a different direction in the future.

6. Others could include such factors as business expansion/contraction, business acquisitions/divestitures, succession planning (possibly involving family members), or any other area related to business development that has not been addressed.

How to Complete a Business Development Analysis

Once again, I will use this section primarily for examples. Refer back to Chapter 6 if you need clarification on the approach.

1. What is the critical strategic issue to be addressed? Examples:

Strategic Area	*Critical Issue*
Services/Products	Expansion of the business over the next five years requires the addition of at least four services or products with significant revenue potential.
Clients/Customers/Mkts.	Expansion of the business over the next five years requires concentration on significantly increasing market share in three high-potential market segments.

Business operations	Expansion of the business over the next five years requires two additional offices in strategic business locations.

2. What data do you have or need to validate this issue and to come up with effective ways of addressing it? If it represents a problem situation, what are the root causes? For example, in order to validate the above issue related to Services/Products, data could include recent sales records of existing services and products, identification of current and potential clients where additional services or products would enhance your position, and a description of additional services or products that could be added without significant investment (The Appendix Worksheets on Service/Product Asessemnt should help in this). Also, your data may suggest that one or more "stand alone" products may have more profit potential than additional services, particularly since these products might not require your professional time in order for the client to purchase and use them. On the other hand, that may defeat your purpose if you wish to have more billable time with your clients.

3. What conclusions and/or alternative courses of action will effectively address the resolution of this issue? For example, if the issue under Services/Products, "Business expansion over the next five years requires the addition of at least four services or products with significant revenue potential," is still valid, appropriate conclusions might be:

a. We need to do a market survey to determine which services or products have the highest potential.

b. We need to assess our current and potential capabilities including investment required to expand them in line with survey results.

c. We need to establish an implementation plan that ensures positive cash flow during the expansion period.

Alternative courses of action, as identified through the use of the related Appendix Worksheets, may focus on one particular service or product that could be introduced fairly quickly and inexpensively thus generating cash flow to underwrite the development of other services or products which may take longer to position.

Examples of Data Analysis

Bill Yancey has been a business consultant for two years, having started his own practice after spending several years on the staff of a major business consulting firm. He realizes he needs a long range marketing and sales plan if he is going to build and maintain his practice. Dr. Robert Moncrief has been a practicing chiropractor for four years and has discovered he has the capability, if he can develop additional means of service delivery, to effectively market his chiropractic services and build the largest and most profitable practice in his area. Dorothy Miller, a public relations professional in private practice for the past six years, recognizes the need for expanded office facilities and additional professional and support staff if she is to achieve her business growth goals.

Figure 8.5: CRITICAL ISSUE ANALYSIS OF BUSINESS DEVELOPMENT AREAS

Bill Yancey, Business Consultant (two years)
Married, 42 years of age, came from a major consulting firm

Critical Issue

I need a long range marketing and sales plan to build and maintain my business.

Supporting Data

● Current clients are primarily ones that followed me from the previous company where I worked, or ones that have come by personal referral.

- The number of clients has remained level for the past year, as has my income.

- I have the capacity to serve several additional clients.

- I have no organized plan for securing additional clients.

Conclusions

- I must develop and implement a long range marketing and sales plan that includes annual growth goals and business diversification plans.

- I need to engage the services of a marketing consultant to assist me.

- Alternative forms of marketing could include:

  - Advertising in the Yellow Pages
  - Classified advertising in newspapers
  - Display or classified advertising in local business journals
  - Joining the Chamber of Commerce and/or one or more service clubs
  - Speaking on my specialty at nearby Chambers and/or service clubs
  - Mailing advertising literature to selected prospects on a regular schedule
  - Sending a personally-developed newsletter to clients and prospects
  - Subscribing to a business newsletter which can be imprinted and mailed to clients and prospects
  - Actively seeking more referrals from current clients
  - Writing a column in a local newspaper
  - Writing and publishing a book or manual to further establish my credibility

---

Dr. Robert Moncrief, Chiropractor (four years)
Married, 33 years of age, 2 children

Critical Issue

Business growth plans indicate a need for additional service delivery capability in the future.

Supporting Data

- Business has been growing at an annual rate of more than 25% for the past two years.

- This growth has come partially as a result of my active participation in the Chamber of Commerce and my numerous speaking engagements at service clubs and other civic groups (which I enjoy very much).

- I am close to service delivery capacity by myself now.

- There is potential for considerably more business in this and nearby communities.

Conclusions

- I have the opportunity to build the largest and most profitable chiropractic practice in the area provided I can develop additional service delivery capability.

- Alternative means of service delivery could include:
  - Additional full time licensed chiropractors
  - Part time licensed chiropractors (subcontracting services from their own practice)
  - Part-time interns from the local chiropractic college
  - Full or part time para-professional employees
  - Opening additional offices (with centralized business services)
  - Merging with or acquiring another chiropractic practice

- I will continue and expand my high visibility activities (speaking, community service, etc.) as a means of further building my business.

Dorothy Miller, Public Relations Professional in Private Practice (Six Years). Divorced, 52 years of age, no children at home

Critical Issue

Business growth plans indicate a need for expanded office facilities including increased data processing capability and additional professional and support staff.

Supporting Data

- Business has been growing approximately 20% per year for the past three years and is projected at the same growth rate for the next three years.

- Two personal computers currently being used are at or close to capacity and are unable to use some of the more sophisticated software programs available for my practice.

- Current staff, other than myself, includes an account executive who plans to retire in two more years, a part-time graphic artist ("moonlighting" from a full-time job), and a part-time receptionist/clerical support person.

- Growth plans will require at least two more full-time account executives, a full-time graphic artist, and a full-time receptionist/clerical person within the next two to three years.

- Current office facilities will not accommodate this expansion; our lease expires in nine months.

Conclusions

- We need to locate and contract for different office facilities that will accommodate our expansion needs including the prospect of additional future expansion.

- We need to select and contract for expanded computer capability in time for our move to new facilities.

- We need to identify specific qualifications for additional staff and establish a schedule for recruiting such staff in line with future needs.

- We need to secure financing to underwrite expansion costs.

Exercise – Developing Your Business Development Analysis

If you are now or expect to be in private practice, or are in a position in your organization that requires attention to business development issues, then working a few critical issues may be an important step in developing your strategic plan. Once again, make copies of the worksheet entitled "Critical Issue Analysis of Business Development Areas" (in the Appendix) and insert them into your Strategic Planning Notebook. Then, identify the one, two or three issues you intend to analyze and proceed to complete a separate sheet for each issue. Be sure to include any additional information you may need to secure and take advantage of outside help.

In Summary

For the professional in private practice, the full spectrum of business development is one that frequently does not get the attention it deserves. In addition to the obvious categories related to the services and/or products you are now or should be offering, the types of clients, customers and markets you should be targeting, and the development of marketing and sales plans, don't forget to take a hard look at the area of associates and staffing and the myriad of factors under business operations that could get you into serious trouble if they don't get highlighted somewhere in your strategic plan.

CHAPTER 9

Strategic Analysis of Financial Areas

THERE ARE FINANCIAL IMPLICATIONS to any strategic decision you might make. Therefore, it is important to identify those financial areas that need to be incorporated into your personal strategic plan. While financial return is important, there are other factors that probably play a much more significant role in the pursuit of your profession. Therefore, this approach to addressing financial issues will be more a means to an appropriate end, and a factor that can be used in measuring that end, than a result you are looking for.

Financial Areas to Consider

1. Cash flow is defined as "having sufficient financial resources available to meet your current requirements." In other words, your income from whatever source has to be at least as much as your expenses. While this is an obvious and fundamental issue, many professionals proceed with their personal planning as though it didn't matter. Whether your income comes from salary, commissions, fees, retainers, product sales, cash reserves, loans, or cash from investors, you need to estimate how much will be available to you at any given time and the degree of assurance you have about its continued flow. Part of your plan needs to include a method of monitoring your income so you can be better prepared to cope with any significant deviations.

Your expenses also need to be identified ahead of time so you can anticipate how they will compare with your projected income. A very simple budget can be prepared that will keep both income and expense sufficiently visible so you can know when significant problems may be developing.

There is nothing more discouraging for a professional than to be on the brink of a major move forward only to discover that cash flow will not support that move. If cash flow management is an area in which you have not been particularly adept in the past, you will need to address that in your strategic plan. This does not necessarily mean that you have to do it personally. There are professionals with skills in that area who can be retained to help you deal with your cash flow. Even so, you will need to be involved in the process.

2. Capital requirements could include such things as: cash required to invest in or purchase an existing practice, office facility requirements, equipment (hardware and software) needed to operate the business, start-up costs (these will almost always be significantly higher than anticipated), image creation (stationery, promotional literature, advertising, even your automobile and clothing if you plan to call on potential clients), underwriting cash flow while the business is getting established or any part of the business that will require a significant one-time cash outlay rather than an ongoing expenditure.

In most cases it is neither necessary nor desirable to meet all capital requirements at the outset of business. Many professionals will start out operating from their homes (and many will continue doing that throughout their professional careers) using borrowed, rented or leased equipment and very simple image creation materials. Having too glitzy an operation before you have established a track record in what you are doing can actually turn off some potential clients, who may perceive your operation as more show than substance.

Capital requirements, of course, can be met from a wide variety of sources including cash reserves, loans, investors, and joint efforts with other professionals. You need to be candid with yourself, of course, as you draw the distinction between what you *must* have and what would be nice to have.

3. Pricing and gross/net profit are important consider-ations. There is an old gag in sales about "losing a dollar on every item sold but making it up on volume." While the absur-dity of that comment is obvious, many professionals, particu-larly when starting out, set their fees or prices for services without a clear concept of what their costs will be or what represents a fair return for the services provided. To a certain degree, the marketplace will determine what is a fair and reasonable fee range to consider. To be competitive, your fee range has to be reasonably comparable to that of other similar professionals unless what you have to offer represents a clear and significant added value. Yet, it is not uncommon to find two professionals of comparable abilities who charge essen-tially the same fees with one retaining a much larger proportion as gross or net profit than the other.

Very simply, gross profit is determined by deducting all direct costs of providing a service from the fees, salary or commissions received from the client or employer. Direct costs include such things as materials, related travel and living expenses, preparation time, delivery and follow-up, cost of support services, and any others that can be directly associated with the delivery of that particular service. Determining net profit would also factor in a portion of fixed and other costs of doing business that are not directly related to that specific service delivery. These include such things as rent, utilities, administrative support, debt servicing, equipment amortiza-tion and taxes.

As you establish what you should be receiving for your services, whether salary, commissions, fees, or retainers, you need to approach that from two perspectives: what the market-place is prepared to pay for someone with your level of exper-tise, and your actual cost of doing business. While, in some ways, this is short term or operational planning, it has strong strategic implications if you anticipate receiving an increased level of compensation in the future.

One of the problems that many professionals have when they go into private practice is, after establishing a particular fee structure at the outset, they fail to make increases that reflect both added value to the client and increased costs. It is not inappropriate to establish a lower fee initially while you develop your business and establish your credibility. This can be seen as an investment in the future. However, at some point, realistic adjustments will have to be made.

4. Net worth is, typically, one of the financial indicators that professionals will look at over a period of time. Net worth, of course, is total personal assets less total personal liabilities. Presumably, one of your desired outcomes would be registering an increase in personal net worth on a continuing basis over the next several years. This is equally applicable whether you are a professional working for someone else, as a part of a professional services firm or in private practice. While a natural progression in personal net worth is a reasonable expectation, it is more useful as a tool for strategic planning if you set your sights on specific milestones you intend to reach; then adjust your short term or operational plans, so that each year you will be able to make the appropriate contributions toward building your net worth.

Your assets can include such things as current receivables, savings, investments, property, retirement fund accumulations, passive income, residual royalties and commissions, and the value of your professional practice. Your liabilities include current payables, indebtedness, business losses, investor equity, and future financial commitments that you have made.

There is nothing wrong with accumulating a certain amount of debt; it is a normal expectation for anyone building a business or a life. However, common sense suggests that whenever liabilities are incurred, there should be either current or future asset acquisition that will at least offset the liability. Establishing a target for increasing your net worth by an average of five to fifteen percent per year over the next several years (net worth planning) may turn out to be one of the more productive ways in which you can build your financial security, while also enhancing your ability to practice your profession more effectively.

5. Cash reserves are related to both cash flow and capital requirements; however it may be a crucial enough area to flag as a separate critical strategic issue. This is especially true if you are anticipating going into private practice at some time in the foreseeable future. As indicated earlier, you may wish to project ahead to determine the cash reserves that will be required to handle the start-up of your practice, including investment in or purchase of an existing practice if that is appropriate, plus the amount you will need in reserve to cover your operating and living costs for the first year. My suggestion is that you estimate this on the high side to cover the inevitable unexpected expenses that come along.

You will be in a far stronger position to put the effort necessary into building a practice if you have had the foresight to establish sufficient reserves so that cash flow and capital requirements are not overriding concerns. Does this mean you should never embark on a start-up operation without having all the cash reserves necessary? Of course not! Opportunities or circumstances may propel you into such a situation before you have accumulated sufficient reserves. However, if you can avoid or minimize the necessity to seek other funds to underwrite your start-up operation, that will certainly ease the operating pressure you will be under.

6. Investments represent a financial area that deserves consideration on all career paths. Investments, of course, can be used as cash reserves when making any significant career move. However, assuming that most professionals will receive higher than average incomes during their careers, one of their concerns will be how to establish a regular plan for saving and investing money in excess of what is needed for ongoing operating and living expenses. There are many resources available that provide excellent guidance in establishing a planned approach to investing available funds (see Bibliography). Therefore, I will not attempt to deal with investment methodologies other than to identify it as a critical strategic area.

7. Acquisitions/Divestitures may be an important area for you some time during your career. Acquisitions can be addressed from two perspectives: as a means of starting up or expanding a private professional practice and as a form of revenue-producing investment. As with investments, there are many publications that provide excellent guidance in evaluating and acquiring existing businesses. Conversely, if you are at a more mature point in your career or are considering another career change, you may also wish to consider establishing plans for divesting yourself of part or all of your business.

8. Others could include such things as: preparing a business to go public, buy-lease-rent decisions, tax planning, and family business involvement as well as personal considerations such as vacations, purchasing or modifying a home, and supporting children or other family members.

Our purpose here is to highlight some of the potential financial areas with the expectation that you will select those issues that will have the most impact on your future. You will undoubtedly have at least one, but my recommendation is that you select *no more than three* critical financial issues or you are likely to get the planning process too biased on the financial side. Remember, entering an issue into your strategic plan does not prevent you from putting effort into other areas that may not be included in the plan. Critical issues enable you to focus on those areas that require the greatest effort.

How to Complete a Strategic Financial Analysis

Here are some examples using the analysis process introduced in Chapter 6.

1. What is the critical strategic issue to be addressed?
Examples:

Strategic Area	Critical Issue
Cash flow	Projected income over the next three years does not provide sufficient margin over projected expenses to both handle contingencies and build a sufficient cash reserve.
Capital requirements	We will need X dollars available by January [year] to cover start-up costs on our new business.

Investments   We need to have sufficient funds
                                available, starting in [year], to cover
                                higher education costs for our
                                children.

2. What data do you have or need to validate this issue and to come up with effective ways of addressing it? If it represents a problem situation, what are the root causes? For example, in order to validate the issue related to Cash Flow, necessary data are projected income from all related sources and projected expenses in all related categories. What you may also want to identify are contingencies related to both income and expense (such as additional revenue opportunities and the potential for unexpected expenses), line items where incremental adjustment in either income or expense is possible with careful planning, estimates of economic conditions that could positively or adversely affect income or expense, and alternative ways of dealing with certain expense items.

Also, your data may suggest that you have overlooked some significant sources of income which may make margin (the difference between income and expense) less of a problem. The issue may then become something like "We need to significantly expand our efforts in X segment in order to meet our income requirements for the future." You also should make certain that you either have or can get the information needed to come up with meaningful conclusions, objectives, and workable plans of action.

3. What conclusions and/or alternative courses of action will effectively address the resolution of this issue? For example, if the issue originally identified under Cash Flow, "Projected income over the next three years does not provide sufficient margin over projected expenses to both handle contingencies and build a sufficient cash reserve," is still valid, appropriate conclusions might be:

a. Projected margins between income and expense
   must be increased by a minimum of 20% per year
   for the next three years until a margin of X is
   reached and maintained thereafter.

b. New potential sources of income need to be identified and activated.

c. Expense items with high dollar impact or with potential for wide fluctuation need to be identified, monitored on a regular basis, and specific courses of action initiated to keep them in line with the results needed.

Additional sources of income might come from new market segments, new products or services, provision of additional value (for an additional fee) to existing clients, joint ventures with other organizations or individuals, or, if you are currently an employee, opportunities for "moonlighting" income. Expense items that may need to be addressed could include buy-lease-rent-borrow options on equipment, advertising and promotion, and staffing versus contracted services among others.

Examples of Data Analysis

The first example is one on personal cash flow as developed by Mark Bellows, a systems analyst with a major insurance company. He and his wife are planning to start a family within the next few years and they have been having trouble just making ends meet. Mary Trent, an attorney within an established law firm, wants to triple her net worth in order to position herself to become a partner in her current firm or with another one. Linda Harkness, a communications consultant who has been in private practice for two years, needs to raise her fees but is concerned about the possible loss of some of her clients if she does. Please look at these as examples only and not as prescriptive ways to address the identified issues. You may have similar issues for which a distinctly different analysis may be more useful.

Figure 9.1: CRITICAL ISSUE ANALYSIS OF FINANCIAL AREAS

Mark Bellows, Systems Analyst with an Insurance Company
Married, 28 years of age, no children

Critical Issue

Personal cash flow needs to be increased incrementally in order to meet anticipated future needs

Supporting Data

- Normal monthly expenses for the past year have nearly equalled monthly income with little or nothing left over for extraordinary expenses or savings.
- Joint income (wife and self) from employers has increased 12% over past year; personal expenses have risen at about the same rate.
- Reserve funds in savings have increased just 10% over the past two years.
- We have decided we would like to start a family within the next three years.

Root Causes

- We do not operate under a personal budget.
- Income has been limited to salaries from employers.
- We purchased a new car within the past year.
- We tend to make purchase decisions impulsively.
- We have postponed having a family during the first five years of marriage, waiting until we were "established" financially.

Conclusions

- We need to establish a personal budget and stick to it.
- We need to develop supplemental sources of income. Alternatives:
  - "Moonlighting" on another job
  - Doing contract work at home

- Teaching at a local college or university
- Establishing a mail order business at home
- We need to build a cash reserve sufficient to cover income loss and increased expenses during the first year following childbirth.

Mary Trent, Attorney with Medium Sized Law Firm
Single, 35 years of age

Critical Issue

Personal net worth needs to be increased significantly on an annual basis in order to reach desired future financial positioning.

Supporting Data

- Personal net worth has been virtually flat for the past three years.
- Approximately three times current net worth is needed to position me to become a partner in this or another law firm.

Root Causes

- I purchased a home last year and had to do some repair and remodeling work to bring it up to the level I found desirable.
- Personal investment portfolio has grown only at about the rate of inflation.
- I will need to make a financial investment in the firm once I am invited to become a partner.

Conclusions

- Home should appreciate in value over the next several years.
- I need to increase my billing rates in line with firm policy.
- I need to significantly increase the amount of money set aside for investment.
- I need to make substantive changes in my investment portfolio and monitor performance on a regular basis.

Linda Harkness, Communications Consultant in Private Practice (two years). Married, 44 years of age, two teenage children

Critical Issue

Current average fees are insufficient to support long term growth and profitability.

Supporting Data

- Fees have not been raised since setting up practice two years ago.
- Fees are below the industry norm for comparable experience.
- Cash flow has reached break even status this year after operating at a loss during the first year.
- Client bookings are at about 80% of current capacity.
- I provide my own clerical and other support services.

Root Causes

- Low fees were established in order to get the business started.
- Husband's income has been sufficient to cover our personal needs until now.
- I have been reluctant to raise fees for fear of losing some current clients.
- Requirement to provide my own support services has limited the amount of time available for client work.
- Business income has not been sufficient to justify hiring support staff.

Conclusions

- I need to establish a plan for gradually raising my fees over the next three years.
- I need to reach agreement with my current clients related to the added value provided and the need to increase my fees accordingly.
- I need to develop and implement a marketing plan de-

signed to attract new clients at the higher fee structure, partially to replace any current clients lost as a result of increased fees.

● I need to hire and train a part-time support person to relieve me of some office responsibilities so I can concentrate more on marketing and delivery of services.

Exercise – Developing Your Financial Analysis

As in previous chapters, you need to start by making several copies of the worksheet "Critical Issue Analysis of Financial Areas" (in the Appendix) and inserting them in your Strategic Planning Notebook. Next, identify one, two or three (I recommend no more than three) critical strategic issues in the financial area that will have a major impact on where you want to be at some point in the future. Reviewing the way you completed "Selecting Your Areas of Strategic Concern," Figure 5.2 on page 78, may help you establish a clear focus. You will need to be much more specific, however, as shown in the explanations and examples in this chapter. Write down each specific issue on a separate worksheet and complete as much of it as you can based on your current knowledge, making sure to include any additional data you may need. Getting someone else to help you with this analysis will increase the likelihood that you have not overlooked critical factors and that you have been reasonably objective in your analysis. Remember, the primary purpose of this step of the process is to make certain you have identified and validated the *right* issue, not to develop a definitive plan of action to address it.

In Summary

Most critical strategic financial issues will fall under the general headings of cash flow, capital requirements, pricing and gross/net profit, net worth, cash reserves, investments, and acquisitions/divestitures. The key is to select those issues that will have the greatest impact on your personal and professional future and to be sure that you have enough information to develop appropriate long term objectives and strategic action plans.

CHAPTER 10

Positioning Yourself with Long Term Objectives

THIS IS THE FIRST TIME in the strategic planning process where we identify specific measurable results in support of the strategic thinking addressed in earlier chapters. While the latter are most important in getting a clear focus, we must now establish specific targets that will *measure* our success in carrying out our strategy. This is where long term objectives come in.

What Do You Want to Have or Become?

Long term objectives, while measurable, differ from most short term goals or objectives in that they establish a position to be attained rather than measurable steps along the way. Most long term objectives will be preceded by the verbs "to have" or "to become." For example:

- To have obtained my CPA by June [year].
- To have sufficient financial reserves in place to enable me to go into full time private practice by January [year].
- To become a partner in a professional services firm by January [year].
- To have a minimum of five articles accepted for publication in appropriate professional journals by September [year].
- To become president of the local chapter of my professional association by June [year].

● To have a minimum of five "bread and butter" clients, with a minimum of $X in annual billings, under contract by January [year].
● To have a minimum of one week per quarter set aside for vacation beginning in [year].

Notice that each of these examples represents a position to be attained rather than an action to be taken. In some cases the action required to reach the objective is fairly obvious while in others there may be a wide variety of ways. Long term objectives provide tangibility, however, to what otherwise might be considered a fuzzy wish list.

How Do You Select Your Highest Priority Objectives?

It would be relatively easy to identify a large number of long term objectives that might be appropriate for your own strategic plan. However, we have found that concentrating on a select few that are likely to have high impact on your strategic direction is much more useful. Typically, somewhere between six and eight long term objectives represent realistic and achievable targets. It may even be appropriate, in the initial stages of your strategic planning process, to concentrate on no more than three or four.

As a starting point, you may wish to go back over your list of Areas of Strategic Concern evaluated in Figure 5.2 on page78. Also, reviewing the analyses you went through in Chapters Six through Nine may help you pinpoint the strategic areas where long term objectives will have the greatest payoff for you. Initially, establish a list of as many strategic areas as may be relevant for you. Conceivably, you could have as many as 15 or 20.

Your next task in prioritization would be to eliminate any areas that are of minor importance or could be combined with others. If you still have a larger number than you can effectively address at the present time, you may wish to use the Decision Matrix described in Chapter Three (a blank reproducible version of which is in the Appendix) to determine which of these areas should have the highest priority. You may have identified some, for example, that are extremely important in terms of your long term direction but which might not require significant attention during the first two or three years of your plan. This might include such things as financing for a business, national or international affiliations, or professional certification of some sort. By retaining these as areas for future consideration, they can be activated at an appropriate time in the future when some of your other objectives have been largely completed.

Figure 10.1 is a worksheet (a blank version is included in the Appendix) with several examples of long term objectives drawn from previous illustrations. This will give you an idea of what long term objectives look like and how they are derived.

Figure 10.1: LONG TERM OBJECTIVES FORMULATION

Selection Process

1. Identify strategic areas that need to be considered for potential long term objectives. Determine which are the six to eight most important.

2. Identify, within each area, the potential results that will move you closer to the fulfillment of your mission. These results should be broad in scope and highly visible.

3. Select and reach consensus, with others who are affected, on no more than six to eight long term objectives that will enable you to be positioned where you want to be at some point in the future. Where possible, write them in an objectives format: "To have (or become) [the result] by [year]."

    Strategic Areas   *Long Term Objectives*

How Do You Validate Your Objectives?

Long term objectives generally start out as preliminary statements; they may be based largely on your desires rather than any assurance that they can be accomplished. Therefore, you need to check each objective statement against some or all of the following criteria:

1. Is it measurable or verifiable? Will you, and others who have a vested interest in its outcome, be able to recognize it when it happens? For example, an objective statement "to become recognized as one of the five leading experts in my area of competence" needs to have some form of measurement such as formal peer recognition in your professional association or entry on a list of preferred service providers by a recognized industry referral service. Also, information on the competition needs to be readily available.

2. Is it achievable or feasible? There is no point in establishing an objective that is clearly beyond reach. Are there major efforts or significant changes that can make reaching the objective achievable? What is the likelihood of these happening? Answering these questions may require addressing such issues as personal skills and abilities, financial resources, other priorities, and the impact of competition or of outside influences. It may be that a strategic action plan for that objective needs to be developed before you can fully determine whether that objective is feasible or achievable.

3. Is it flexible or adaptable? Because there are unknown factors, whatever objective you set must be flexible enough to take into account changing circumstances and new opportunities. For example, a five-year objective "to become a principal" in a particular professional services firm is likely to be contingent on a number of separate, but related, factors, such as expansion of the firm's business, your own financial resources, the retirement or separation of other principals, and the competition of other professionals in the firm who may have similar ambitions. As you proceed with your annual updates of your strategic action plan you may reach the conclusion that your target date needs adjusting, that affiliation with another firm or starting your own firm may have greater potential, or that a senior management position, without principal status, may be an equally worthwhile objective. If you lock yourself into a single specific result that does not allow for modification as you proceed, you may be setting yourself up for failure.

4. Is it consistent with the rest of the plan? The whole purpose of the earlier steps in the planning process is to provide a firm basis for your future decision-making. If the long term objective you are considering does not make a significant contribution to what you have established earlier, you need to either change your objective or go back and review your earlier strategic decisions to determine if they are still valid. The strategic planning process, of course, is an iterative one that encourages you to continually review and, when appropriate, modify earlier decisions.

What Do You Do with the "Leftovers?"

In the course of developing your six to eight long term objectives, it is highly conceivable and, in fact, likely that you will have identified several other worthwhile targets to shoot for. You don't want to lose sight of these objectives. They may be worthy of your attention either in future strategic plans or, possibly, in your annual operational plan. My suggestion is that you set up a separate page to be included in your planning notebook called "Alternative Long Term Objectives" or "Objectives for Future Consideration." The same validating criteria that you have applied to your primary objectives may still be used so that you don't create inappropriate diversions. If you happen to be employed within a larger diverse organization or within a professional services firm, you may wish to share these "other" objectives with key people who could affect your future.

Where Do Assumptions Fit in the Planning Process?

You undoubtedly looked at certain assumptions as you went through your strategic analysis. You may find it helpful to list them along with your long term objectives. For example, an objective to "to become a principal" undoubtedly will be affected by assumptions related to volume of business, the perspectives of existing principals, and certain economic factors. An objective within a diverse organization "to have the ability to provide" a particular technical service may depend on such things as state-of-the-art technology, availability of organizational resources, and the support of top management.

When long term objectives are based on assumptions, these assumptions should be included as part of the plan along with the objectives. When assumptions change, the objectives must be re-examined and may have to be revised in light of new information.

Figure 10.2: EXAMPLES OF LONG TERM OBJECTIVES

Barbara Spangler, Electronics Engineer

Strategic Areas	*Long Term Objectives*
Family relations	To have a plan in place by [date] mutually agreed upon with each of my children, for how we will work together when they enter high school.
Health, rest & recreation	To have a minimum of a half day every other week set aside for *me* that is not directly related to either work or family.
Work experience	To become a manager of a multidisciplinary operation in my company by [date].
Cash flow	To have a minimum monthly net cash flow of $X next year, increasing to $Y the following year.

Cash reserves	To have a minimum of $X in cash reserves (liquid investments) by [date], increasing by a minimum of 5% each quarter thereafter.

Jack Michaels, Accountant

Strategic Areas	*Long Term Objectives*
Certification	To become a CPA not later than [date].
Cash reserves	To have a minimum of $X in reserve (to underwrite start-up costs of my business) by [date].
Career path	To become an accountant in private practice not later than [date].
Clients	To have a minimum of X clients on retainer by the end of my first year of operation in private practice.
Cash flow	To have a minimum monthly cash flow of $X by the end of my first year of operation.
Family involvement	To have my wife as a full-time partner in my business by [date].
Service	To allocate a minimum of X hours per month for service to my church and to the YMCA beginning not later than my second year in private practice.

Figure 10.3: GENERIC EXAMPLES OF LONG TERM OBJECTIVES

Strategic Areas	*Long Term Objectives*
Cash flow	To have a minimum monthly cash flow of $10,000 by January [year].

Capital requirements	To have a minimum of $50,000 available for investment in my business by September [year].
Pricing, gross/net profit	To have a minimum average gross profit on services of 50% beginning in [year].
Net worth	To have a minimum net worth of $400,000 by [year], increasing a minimum of 10% annually thereafter.
Education	To have passed the California Bar Examination by [year].
Certification	To become a CSP (Certified Speaking Professional) by [year].
Research/Study	To have completed a funded study of [technical area] by June [year].
Publications	To have a technical book completed and accepted for publication by December [year].
Affiliations	To become an adjunct professor at Northwestern University by [year].
Work experience	To have a minimum of two years' management experience in my technical field by [year].
Services/Products	To have at least one proprietary product in my technical field available for sale and distribution by [year].
Clients/Customers/Mkts	To become an acknowledged resource in at least three federal agencies by [year].
Marketing/Sales	To become actively affiliated with at least five marketing/sales outlets by [year].

Associates/Staffing	To have an active mutually-supportive working relationship with at least three other professionals by [year].
Business operations	To have a part-time office manager on staff by September [year], moving toward a full-time position within two years.
Family/Personal relations	To have an annual planning "advance" (a more positive term than "retreat") with my family, beginning this summer to plan and implement a program of family-involvement activities.
Health, rest & recreation	To have a complete physical examination at least every two years, beginning this year, leading to establishment of a regular health improvement plan.
Cultural pursuits	To become a member of the violin section of our community orchestra by [year].
Service	To serve on two ongoing boards or committees in our church or community each year, beginning this year.

Exercise – Developing Your Long Term Objectives.

Making copies of the worksheet "Long Term Objectives Formulation" (in the Appendix) for use in your Strategic Planning Notebook may be very helpful for your continued planning efforts. On this worksheet, list those strategic areas that you have selected as the ones on which you wish to set long term objectives at this time. Then, using some of the data generated in your earlier analysis, identify objectives that will represent significant positions to be attained in the future.

Normally, your long term objectives will represent positions that will require more than one year to attain. I recommend that you limit your objectives to only those where you are ready and willing to make a significant commitment toward their achievement. Initially, this could be no more than two or three. After you have these established clearly, you may wish to seek the advice of others who can give you effective feedback.

In Summary

Long term objectives represent the first step in the strategic planning process that focuses on specific measurable results. They differ from most short term goals or objectives because they concentrate on positions to be attained rather than specific accomplishments. Frequently they are preceded by the verbs "to have" or "to become." The analysis you went through with your critical issues in Chapters Six through Nine, particularly the conclusions reached, should provide you with the information you need to formulate your own long term objectives. For most people, six to eight long term objectives is about the maximum, but it may be appropriate to focus on no more than three or four.

Once you have identified the objectives you want to include in your plan, you need to validate each of them by asking the following questions: Is it measurable or verifiable? Is it achievable or feasible? Is it flexible or adaptable? Is it consistent with the rest of the plan? Once you have clearly formulated your long term objectives or positions to be attained, then you are ready to proceed with your strategic action plans to determine how best to get there.

CHAPTER 11

Making the Future a Reality Through Strategic Action Plans

UP TO THIS POINT we have been concentrating primarily on creating the concepts, direction, and eventual positions to be attained if the future we are designing is to become a reality. However, all the concepts and ideas in the world are of little value unless they are translated into specific actions at some point. That's where strategic action plans come in. They create the means by which our long term objectives can be reached. Without them, we are likely to be positioned forever in "never-never land." "Wishing will make it so" only happens in the movies.

We now take the step in the strategic planning process that helps us assess the wide variety of alternative actions available to us, the advantages and disadvantages of each, the time and resources necessary to carry them out, the support needed from others, and the personal effort required on our own part to ensure that we are proceeding in a manner that is likely to make our efforts a success.

What Kinds of Action Plans are Most Likely to Help You Achieve Your Long Term Objectives?

Basically, there are only three kinds of actions plans that can help you achieve either long term or short term objectives. They are:

1. A series of activities or events, the carrying out of which will, collectively, lead to the accomplishment of your objective. These activities or events are not necessarily inter-connected. For example, a long term objective "to become recognized as one of the top five experts in my field in my service area by [year]" could include any or all of the following activities or events:

- Being retained professionally by some of the top companies in the area.

- Providing specific volunteer or paid professional services to community agencies.

- Becoming listed with specific referral services.

- Becoming a leader in the local chapter of your professional association.

- Completing certification and/or receiving formal recognition from peers.

2. An analytical or problem-solving approach which incorporates a series of *interconnected* activities or events. This involves the traditional problem-solving methodology which includes identifying the problem or situation, analyzing and assessing alternative ways of addressing it, and developing and implementing appropriate solutions. For example, an information systems professional in charge of a unit within an organization's Management Information Systems Department might state a long term objective as "to have a completely automated project reporting system in place and functioning by [year]." Assuming that the complexity of this particular situation is one that will require two or more years to effectively implement, here are the steps, with target dates to be added, that might reasonably be followed in attaining the objective:

- Identify the need for the service – including relative costs (time and money) of the current system compared to the proposed system, relative accuracy of information, fixing and tracking of accountability for performance and re-sponsiveness to the customer, etc.

- Determine system requirements – hardware, software and personnel, including the cost and time required for acquisition.
- Establish the proposed implementation plan, including the orientation or training of related organization personnel and customers.
- Gain the agreement and commitment (including funding), plus formal approval where necessary, of all those who will be directly affected.
- Implement the acquisition plan.
- Conduct a pilot implementation effort with one or more units in order to test and modify the system.
- Implement the system.
- Follow up on a regularly scheduled basis to evaluate system usage, make modifications as appropriate, and establish ongoing maintenance and productivity targets.

3. A series of smaller or shorter term objectives that will break the total plan down into more bite sized pieces which can be prioritized and incorporated into subsequent annual operating plans. For example, an employee within a professional services firm might have a long term objective "to become a principal or partner within this firm by [year]." Following is a list of possible shorter term objectives which might progressively lead to the desired ultimate objective:

- Become a project leader within six months.
- Become a designated liaison with three or more specific clients within one year.
- Be responsible for the acquisition of a minimum of $X in new business for the firm within 18 months.
- Become a district manager within two years.
- Become an officer within four years.
- Become a principal or partner within six years.

Each of these smaller or shorter term objectives, of course, will require its own specific action plan to insure its completion.

Also, recognize that the time frames identified may need to be adjusted periodically to reflect current circumstances.

How Do You Get Started with Strategic Action Plans?

Once you have decided on your long term objectives, the first step is to identify alternative ways of working towards each one. There are very few objectives that can be reached in only one way. Therefore, we suggest that you not limit yourself to the first alternative that comes to mind. Rather, let your mind flow freely and try to identify as many different alternatives as possible. One technique that works well is what I call the Alternative Evaluation Chart, as illustrated in Figure 11.1. This is a technique that can be used in any kind of decision-making situation where multiple criteria are used in the evaluation. However, I have found it especially useful in assessing and evaluating alternative courses of action when working towards the accomplishment of an objective.

Identify as many possibilities as you can think of, regardless of whether or not they might be used. This works most effectively using a brainstorming process. While this can be done individually, it is generally more productive when it involves two or more concerned people, when a synergy frequently takes place as different people's ideas come together. Also, an impractical idea will often stimulate thought leading to another idea which may be worth considering.

For example, we have Alan Curtis (a management consultant with an office in the home and a part-time office assistant) who is currently generating approximately $60,000 gross revenue per year with an average of eight billing days per month. A long term objective has been established "to have a minimum of $150,000 in annual revenue within three years." Recognizing that several days a month need to be allocated to marketing and sales, non-billable development efforts, administration, and personal time, there are, at most, four to six additional billable days of Alan's time available each month. The following (Figure 11.1) is a list of the alternatives he has considered, with the aid of some colleagues.

Figure 11.1: ALTERNATIVE EVALUATION CHART EXAMPLE
Alan Curtis, Management Consultant

OBJECTIVE: *To have a minimum of $150,000 in annual revenue within three years.*

ALTERNATIVES	Impact	Cost	Can I	Will I	Timing	Notes
Write book	M	M-H	M-H	M	Long	Work on for future
~~Buy another practice~~	M	H	L	L	—	—
Sell products:						
• self-published	M	M-H	M-H	M	Medium	Good potential
• produced by others	M-H	L-M	M-H	M	Short	Excellent potential
Vertical mktg existing clients	M	L	M	H	Short	Excellent potential
Referrals from existing clients	M	L	M	H	Short	Excellent potential
Create consultant coalition	L-M	L	H	M	Medium	Possibility
Broker/finder fees	L-M	L	M	M	Short	Fair potential
~~Hire revenue-producing staff~~	M	H	M	L	—	—
Get revenue-producing assoc.	M	M	M	M	Short	Fair potential
~~Merge with another firm~~	H	H	M	L	—	—
~~Get high visibility assignment~~	M	L-M		L	—	—
~~Better use of computer~~	L				—	—
Become recognized expert	M-H	M	M	M	Long	Work on for future
Establish higher fees	H	L	M	H	Short	Excellent potential
Get speaking engagements	H	L-M	M	M	Medium	Good potential
~~Develop proprietary products~~	H	H	M	L	—	—
~~Get corporate sponsor~~	M	L-M	L		—	—
Publish newsletter:						
~~• subscription~~	M	M-H	M	L	—	—
• free/promotional	M	M	M	M	Medium	Good potential

After listing the alternatives, the next step is to go through the list and eliminate any that are clearly impractical. Then criteria are established against which each of the alternatives will be evaluated. The criteria that I have used most often in this process are: impact on objective (how much will this alternative help you achieve your objective?), cost (of bringing the alternative to fruition), feasibility ("Can I" – do you have or can you get the capability, time and resources required?) and commitment ("Will I" – are you willing to put forth the effort to make it happen?). Additional criteria could include such things as: timing, impact on other objectives, personal preference, or any other that would be relevant to your situation. You are limited here only by your own imagination.

Once your criteria have been established, make an evaluation in each column for each of the alternatives. This could be as simple as rating them High, Medium, or Low. Or, you could use a numerical ranking such as one (Low) to five (High). Another way would be to place each of the alternatives in rank order of importance, as we did with the Decision Matrix.

As you can see, Alan and his colleagues have identified several potential ways for him to achieve his objective of $150,000 in annual revenue within three years. They have chosen to use the rating High, Medium, and Low for their evaluations in the first three columns. Then they added another column representing Timing (to implement the alternative) with Long, Medium, and Short for their evaluations. After eliminating alternatives once a Low evaluation is reached, they ended up with several possibilities including four with excellent potential: selling related products that are produced by others, vertical marketing with existing clients (additional services within the same company), getting referrals to prospects from existing clients, and establishing higher fees (recognizing the need to use care in raising fees with existing clients). Consequently, he has some fairly short term actions he can take plus some that need to be worked on for the future.

How Do You Prepare a Strategic Action Plan?

Once you have decided on the courses of action you intend to follow in reaching your long term objective, your next step is to identify the sequence of activities or events, in the order in which they need to occur, so that you can begin to concentrate your efforts on what needs to be accomplished in the short run as well as to project ahead what needs to take place at designated times in the future. This does not need to be an elaborately detailed action plan. However, it should be such that it is relatively easy to identify significant milestones and to make appropriate modifications in the plan as you proceed.

Figure 11.2 represents a worksheet that can be used for this purpose, as applied to Alan Curtis, the management consultant referred to earlier. Remember it is important to *adapt* this worksheet to your own circumstances so that it will become a living document. Properly completed, it should give you a data base from which you can develop more detailed short term plans. Alan has identified six major strategic action steps designed to position him to receive $150,000 in annual gross revenue in three years. Each step and substep, of course, will need its own short term plan for implementation to ensure that his targets are met, and experience may cause him to modify the specifics as he proceeds.

Exercise – Developing Your Strategic Action Plan

You may wish to make copies of the Alternative Evaluation Chart and the Strategic Action Plan Format (blank versions of which are included in the Appendix) and put them in your Strategic Planning Notebook. Then, use them in connection with one or more of your long term objectives. Using one, or a combination, of the three kinds of action plans covered in this chapter, enter the major steps required and the sequence in which they have to occur in the column marked "What." Since this is a *strategic* action plan, one which should take two or more years to complete, enter in the "When" column the approximate schedule for completing each step by month (or quarter) and year. Sometimes it helps to start by fixing the target date for the objective and working backwards to the present. If it then appears that you cannot achieve the objective within the time frame projected, you may wish to re-evaluate the date for your objective, modify your action plan to make it more achievable, or, possibly, reconsider whether or not the objective is viable at all.

Next, estimate the approximate cost of carrying out that step in the "How Much" column. At the very least, you will want to identify any out-of-pocket costs associated with it. You may also find it useful to estimate the amount of your time and the time of others that may be required. If people other than yourself will be involved in any of your action steps, identify

Figure 11.2: STRATEGIC ACTION PLAN FORMAT

Long Term Objective: To have a minimum of $150,000 in annual gross revenue within three years.
(Current year's revenues = $60,000 as baseline).

What	When	How Much	Who	On Track?
1. Generate minimum additional income from existing clients (Short term action plan needed)				
a. $10,000	Year 1	10 hrs/mo	Alan	Monthly billings
b. $20,000	Year 2	10 hrs/mo	"	" "
c. $30,000	Year 3	10 hrs/mo	"	" "
2. Generate minimum additional income from client referrals (Short term action plan needed)				
a. $10,000	Year 1	20 hrs/mo	"	" "
b. $20,000	Year 2	20 hrs/mo	"	" "
3. $30,000	Year 3	20 hrs/mo	"	" "
3. Generate minimum additional income from increased fees (Short term action plan needed)				
a. $ 5,000	Year 1	Minimum	"	" "
b. $10,000	Year 2	"	"	" "
c. $15,000	Year 3	"	"	" "

4. Generate minimum additional income from product sales (Short term action plan needed)			
a. Identify and contract for products	Yr 1, Qtr 1	40 hrs, $??	Alan/Martha	Distributor contract
b. $ 5,000	Yr 1, balance	15 hrs/mo	Alan	Monthly billing
c. $10,000	Year 2	15 hrs/mo	"	" "
d. $20,000	Year 3	15 hrs/mo	"	" "
5. Write a book and get it published			
a. Determine subject, establish writing plan and outline	Yr 1, Qtr 1	40 hrs	Alan	Plan existence
b. Write at least 3 articles on subject and submit to appropriate journals	Yr 1, Qtr 3	40 hrs	Alan/Martha	Articles submitted
c. Secure agent and/or publisher	Yr 2, Qtr 2	40 hrs	Alan	Agreement signed
d. Complete manuscript	Yr 2, Qtr 4	150 hrs	"	Manuscript compl.
e. Have book published	Yr 3, Qtr 3	100 hrs	"	Book in hand
6. Publish and distribute promotional newsletter			
a. Quarterly thereafter	Yr 2, Qtr 1	100 hrs 20 hrs/Qtr	Alan/Martha " "	Newsletter mailed " "

them in the "Who" column – it may require some special effort on your part to get their support. The "On Track?" column is especially important if you need to have a means of knowing how you are doing on each step. What feedback device will keep you informed?

Developing your strategic action plan is another effective way to get others who are important to your future involved in your strategic planning process.

In Summary

The strategic action plan is the bridge between your long range strategic plan and your short term tactical or operational plan. It is the first time in the process that we have taken a hard look at exactly *how* you are going to achieve the results that are important to your future. There are three, and only three, kinds of action plans for achieving either long term or short term objectives: a series of activities or events, an analytical or problem-solving approach, and a series of smaller or shorter term objectives. Any action plan you establish will be one or a combination of these three kinds. Having determined your long term objectives, you then have to identify the most appropriate way to carry them out and then lay out the specific steps required including the what, when, how much, and who. With the action planning methodology in hand, together with the information generated in each of the other steps, you are now ready to make your future become a reality.

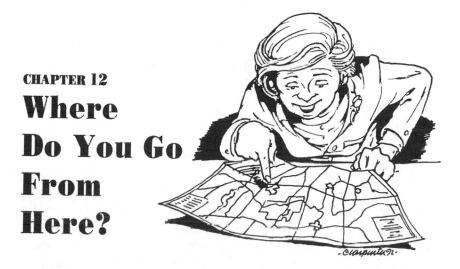

CHAPTER 12

Where Do You Go From Here?

WE'VE TAKEN A LONG and, perhaps, arduous journey through the process of *creating your future*. At this stage you may have mixed feelings. On the one hand, you may have a clearer sense of purpose and direction. On the other, you may have an overwhelming feeling of "system overload" as you have identified the number of actions you could, and perhaps should, be taking. Reality suggests that, if you try to "do it all" right away, you are setting yourself up for failure. Planning efforts are most successful when they are designed to be taken a step at a time and to virtually ensure success at each step along the way. Remember, this is your personal *strategic* plan – one that needs to be implemented over several *years*, not weeks or months. Furthermore, as we have stressed throughout this book, you need to *adapt* this process to your own style and circumstances, not *adopt* it because some guy who wrote a book makes it sound so compelling. A plan, in your personal life or in your business, is only useful if it gets implemented. And that has to be done in a manner that is comfortable, challenging and achievable for you and whoever else is helping in the creation of the plan.

Translating Your Plans Into Action

One way to get started is to make a quick assessment of where you are now in your personal strategic planning process and do some tentative projections as to when it will be appropriate and realistic to concentrate on some of the steps.

Figure 12.1 shows how Barbara Spangler, our engineer, made such an assessment before getting started on her specific actions. As you can see, there are three general headings, Planning Process, Other People Involved, and Implementation, with several specific items listed under each. Then there are six columns for assessment: "N.A." stands for "Not Applicable" and should be checked for any of the items that clearly do not now, nor would ever be likely to, represent something for you to be involved with; a check under "O.K." means that is a step that is currently being addressed reasonably satisfactorily; "Do Now" represents something you should be putting significant effort into immediately, say within the next three months; you would check "This Year" if this represents a step you should complete or have under control within the next 12 months; you would place a check under "Next Year" or "Future" if either of those represents a more realistic time frame. For some items, you may put a check in the "Do Now" and one or more of the three following columns, which would indicate you need to start work on it immediately but do not expect to have it completed until some time in the future.

Included under "Planning Process" are listed the various steps that have been covered at some length in this book, not all of which you will find it necessary to follow. For example, "Organizational Mission" would probably be appropriate only if you are in an executive position or operating a business where that would not be satisfactorily covered under your personal and professional mission. "Other People Involved" gives you the opportunity to identify who else you want to include and at what point they should become involved. "Implementation" includes the identification of specific things that will help you stay on target, such as a "strategic planning notebook" for keeping your plans together so you can work with them and the establishment of graphic displays or charts for keeping your plans visible as you track your progress.

In our illustration, Barbara has addressed her "career path choices" already but will review them next year. She wants to

Figure 12.1: BARBARA SPANGLER'S PLANNING CHECKLIST

	N.A.	O.K.	Do Now	This Year	Next Year	Future
PLANNING PROCESS						
Career path choices		√			√	
Strategic values			√		√	
Personal & professional mission			√			
Organizational mission	√					
Strategic analysis						
Personal			√		√	
Professional growth			√		√	
Business development						?
Financial			√		√	
Long term objectives				√	√	
Strategic action plans				√	√	
Other	√					
OTHER PEOPLE INVOLVED						
Spouse/life partner	√					
Children			√			
Other family	√					
Employer				√		
Professional colleagues				?		
Friends				?		
Facilitator				?		
Other	√					
IMPLEMENTATION						
Strategic planning notebook			√			
Review schedule			√			
Graphic display/charts				?		
Plan modification					√	√
Other	√					

begin work immediately on her "strategic values," "personal and professional mission" and the analysis of selected "personal," "career growth" and "financial" issues both now and next year, with "business development" a consideration for the future, depending on the direction her career takes. She plans to involve her children in her planning process now, and her employer later this year, once she has more clearly defined her priorities. She may or may not wish to involve anyone else. She has decided to start a "strategic planning notebook" which will include a "review schedule" now and will look into the possibility of displaying her plans graphically later this year. She recognizes also the probable need to modify her plans next year and in the future, depending on how they evolve.

Our accountant, Jack Michaels, who is working on his CPA, is illustrated in Figure 12.2. He has completed his "career path choices" and "strategic values," although he wants to review them next year. He sees the necessity to complete his "personal and professional mission" now and will possibly proceed to a separate "organizational mission" when his plans to move out on his own come closer to realization. He wants to analyze selected issues in all four strategic categories now, as he begins to reposition himself, and recognizes that he will have to look at some different "business development" and "financial" issues next year and in the future in preparation for, and following, his move. Jack's wife clearly needs to be involved immediately in his planning and he plans to bring his employer into the picture later this year. He is undecided at this point if and when to include "professional colleagues," "friends" or a "facilitator." He sees a "strategic planning notebook" and "review schedule" as important tools to set up now and will determine later this year if some sort of graphic display will be useful. He also recognizes the likelihood that he will have to modify his plan next year depending on his progress.

If you are ready to make your own assessment, make a copy of "Your Planning Checklist" (in the Appendix). Then complete it, following the directions given above, as best you can from your current frame of reference. (I suggest using a *pencil* rather than a pen as you may wish to change it as you proceed.) Then

Figure 12.2: JACK MICHAEL'S PLANNING CHECKLIST

	N.A.	O.K.	Do Now	This Year	Next Year	Future
PLANNING PROCESS						
Career path choices		√			√	
Strategic values		√			√	
Personal & professional mission			√			
Organizational mission					?	
Strategic analysis						
Personal			√			
Professional growth			√			
Business development			√		√	√
Financial			√		√	√
Long term objectives				√	√	
Strategic action plans				√	√	
Other	√					
OTHER PEOPLE						
Spouse/life partner			√			
Children	√					
Other family	√					
Employer				√		
Professional colleagues				?		
Friends				?		
Facilitator				?		
Other	√					
IMPLEMENTATION						
Strategic planning notebook			√			
Review schedule			√			
Graphic display/charts				?		
Plan modification					√	
Other	√					

review the items you have checked in the "Do Now" column and determine if you can realistically address them all in the near future. If that appears overly ambitious, then prioritize them in the order that makes sense for you.

Setting a Realistic Schedule

Once you have identified the steps in the process you intend to follow, you will want to establish a schedule when each of the steps is to be started, completed or both. If you wish, you can use the Strategic Action Plan Format (in the Appendix) as a tool for identifying each of the steps and an appropriate schedule for each. Another approach would be to take a simple 12-month calendar and insert it into your Strategic Planning Notebook, placing your start and completion points for each step under the appropriate date. (Once again, I suggest using a *pencil* as this is likely to change.) There is also a wide variety of wall-mounted calendars which can be used for this purpose. You will probably find that a calendar with all 12 months visible simultaneously is more useful than one that shows only a month or a quarter at a time.

If you have established a specific date when your strategic plan needs to be completed, as is appropriate in many businesses, scheduling generally works more effectively by starting with the completion date on the calendar and working backwards, figuring the amount of time that will be required to develop each step. If the completion date is not crucial, you may find it easier to project your planning schedule forward, recognizing that you may have to shift the schedule for certain steps, depending on the time needed for each one. It is important to set a schedule as a self-disciplining control. Without a schedule, it is too easy to procrastinate. However, unless your final completion date is fixed, you will be far better off taking whatever time is necessary to complete each step properly rather than adhering to an artificial schedule.

Communicating Your Plans to Others

If others will be actively involved in the determination of your plans, you need to secure their commitment to that process well in advance of when their assistance will be required so they can give it the attention it deserves. Also, while part of their motivation will probably be a desire to help you with your planning, they will be able to support the effort more enthusiastically if they see some personal benefit in that participation. This can range from awareness of where you are going and determining the impact of that on their own efforts to creating complementary plans of their own that might be personally rewarding.

There are probably other people who are important to your future who may not play an active role in the development of your plans but need to be kept informed. These could include members of your family, current or potential employers, current or potential associates or employees, current or potential clients or customers, your banker or potential investors, as well as selected friends and professional colleagues. Sharing your plans with them, either at completion or while they are evolving, can be a powerful way of enlisting their support when it is needed. A well-laid-out plan demonstrates your own commitment to your future and is more likely to get the kind of positive response from others that you want.

Tracking Your Plans

One of the values in having a Strategic Planning Notebook and a planning calendar is that they provide a vehicle for ensuring that you follow through with your commitments. In the initial stages of your strategic planning effort, we recommend setting firm dates, at least once a quarter, when you will take time out to review what you have accomplished – with both the development and implementation of your plan, the assessment of how well you are doing, what modifications need to be made, and where you need to invest more time and effort in order to remain on track. Establishing a plan without a review schedule is like planting seeds in your garden and never watering or nurturing them. Neither is likely to produce the results you want.

When and How to Modify Your Plans

While you will make modifications periodically as a part of your tracking process, you need to formally review your personal strategic plan from top to bottom at least once a year or whenever there is a significant change in your situation. Professional and business opportunities are likely to change, sometimes without your being consciously aware of them. Your personal values and philosophy may need to be revisited as you become more sensitive to their effect on your career and your life. New strategic issues may appear and ones you have been working on may become less critical, suggesting a shift in your priorities. Planning is a dynamic, living process that needs to reflect changing circumstances. It is not a rigid, static process that locks you into a given course of action regardless of what is happening in your world.

One way of taking a fresh look at your strategic plan is to complete the worksheet, "Clarifying Your Personal and Professional Mission," every year or two *as though you did not already have a mission statement or strategic plan*. Merely looking over your existing mission statement, or your answers to the questions as completed originally, has a tendency to confine your thinking. Strategic planning is a creative process; you need to allow your imagination to run freely before beginning to focus on specifics. The same approach is equally useful, and maybe more so, in strategic analysis; you need to make certain that the issues you are addressing are the ones most relevant to where you are going.

In Summary

There is no "right" way to develop and implement your personal strategic plan. It clearly must be adapted to your own specific style and circumstances. You have to assess where you are now, where you want to be, what steps in the process are going to help you get there, and what represents a realistically challenging schedule for making your plan come alive. The active involvement and support of others who are important to your future is also essential. Your plan must be seen, by you and by others, as a dynamic, living document that will guide you in a positive direction while permitting you to adjust your path or even move in a different direction when it makes sense to do so.

Creating Your Future is a way to make your dreams come true while still paying attention to reality. Dream on and then make them happen!

Annotated Bibliography

IFIND A BIBLIOGRAPHY to be more interesting and meaningful if the author comments on why a particular book is included rather than merely listing it. Each book described here (under seven separate categories – Planning for Success, Inspiration, Career Planning, Business Planning, Financial Planning, Home and Family, and Writing/Publishing) has a special contribution to make to the personal strategic planning process. Several have been written by friends and colleagues for whom I have the greatest respect. There are many others I could have included, but these should give you ample food for thought as you continue your journey in Creating Your Future.

Planning for Success

There are literally thousands of books that profess to offer a blueprint for success – some that provide powerful insights and guidance, many that contain little more than platitudes. Here are a few that I have found especially meaningful.

Bramson, Robert M., Ph.D., *Coping with the Fast Track Blues: A Survival Guide for Your Climb to the Top*, New York: Doubleday 1990. If you are, or expect to be, on the fast track to the top in an organization, this book will help you cope with the feelings of depression, anger and resentment that inevitably show up along the way. Bob Bramson, author of the popular book, *Coping with Difficult People*, has come up with a series of tests, programs and specific guidelines to assist you in dealing with the stress associated with being on the fast track in corporate America.

Dahl, Dan and Randolph Sykes, *Charting YOUR Goals: Personal Life-Goals Planner*, New York: Harper & Row 1988. Primarily a personal planning workbook, this is loaded with self-directed exercises that will help you focus on what is important to you. If you like the worksheets in my book, you'll love the ones you will find here.

Ford, George A. and Gordon L. Lippitt, *Creating Your Future: A Guide to Personal Goal Setting*, San Diego, CA: University Associates 1988. I was attracted to this book not only because of the similarity of the title to my book (title independently arrived at) but out of respect for Gordon Lippitt. I had the privilege of sharing the platform and spending some quality time with Gordon about a month before his untimely death in 1985. As with the Dahl and Sykes book, this is in a workbook format that is designed to guide you step by step through a personal growth planning cycle that is different from, but complementary to, my book.

Mackenzie, Alec, *Time For Success: A Goal-Getter's Strategy*, New York: McGraw-Hill 1989. Time is one of those exhaustible commodities we need to master if we are to move ahead personally and professionally. Here, the author of the best-selling book, *The Time Trap*, has put together a primer for making the most effective use of time in our careers and personal lives. Alec's ideas on breaking human, managerial and environmental time barriers are especially helpful.

Mager, Robert F., *Goal Analysis*, Belmont, CA: Lake Publishing Co. 1984. Never out of date, Bob Mager's books are fun to read but, more important, they pack a powerful message in easy-to-understand language. This book is designed to help you take a broad statement of intent and remove it from "the land of Fuzz" so that "you will know one when you see one."

Morrisey, George L., *Getting Your Act Together: Goal Setting for Fun, Health and Profit*, New York: Wiley 1980. This is the real predecessor to my current book. Written in jargon-free language, it shows how you can identify, set, and *achieve* those goals that are most important to you. This book and related cassette learning programs are available from The Morrisey Group (see page xix).

Newman, James W., *Release Your Brakes!*, New York: Warner Books 1977. This classic book on personal growth by the creator of the world-renowned PACE (Personal And Company Effectiveness) Seminar will show you how to release the tremendous potential within you and take charge of your life. Jim's metaphor of driving your car with the brakes on and experiencing the surge of power that comes when those brakes are released sets the stage for a provocative and powerful journey to a fulfilling life.

Qubein, Nido R., *Get the Best from Yourself*, Englewood Cliffs, NJ: Prentice-Hall 1983, Berkeley Books edition 1986. Nido is an incredibly successful businessman and one of the most sought-after professional speakers in America; and this from a man who came to this country in 1966 with no money, no connections and almost no understanding of the English language. His straightforward approach to personal and professional success is chock full of sound concepts and techniques.

Tracy, Brian, *The Psychology of Achievement, The Psychology of Success, How to Start and Succeed in Your Own Business*, Chicago: Nightingale-Conant. These three audiocassette programs are especially appropriate for readers of this book. They are among the best sellers in the Nightingale-Conant catalogue and it's obvious why. Brian has a knack for getting to the heart of what people really need to know to be successful. He is also the editor and host of N-C's popular monthly Insight series. He has influenced the development of many of the ideas included in my book. I heartily recommend anything Brian Tracy produces as being one of your best personal learning experiences.

Inspiration

Out of the countless books that could have been included under the heading of Inspiration, I have selected six that speak to the interests of readers of this book.

Atthreya, N. H., *The You and I in Business and Life: What makes people give their best*, Los Altos, CA: Starsong Publications 1987. I have had the privilege of knowing Nagam Atthreya for more than 20 years, having spent time in his home in Bombay, India, and he in ours. He is one of the foremost management consultants in India whose insights transcend nationality. This is a moving and inspiring book written with a poetic hand.

Batten, Joe D., *Expectations and Possibilities: How to Create Your Path to Discovery and Achievement*, Santa Monica, CA: Hay House 1990. Although better known for his books, *Tough Minded Leadership* and *Tough Minded Management*, this is one of my favorites of Joe's and is an update of an earlier edition. In it, he helps us develop an *expective* attitude toward life and work. This begins with the use of expective words, actions and concepts like – Look forward, Hope, Anticipate and Expand – that provide a positive and productive mental perspective for Creating Your Future.

Briles, Judith, *The Confidence Factor: How Self-Esteem Can Change Your Life*, New York: MasterMedia 1990. Judith has done an incredible job of pulling together the results of a major survey related to confidence within women from all walks of life in a highly informative and entertaining manner. Some results are predictable; others are quite surprising. The book is full of real-people stories that make powerful points. It concludes with "The Ten Commandments of Confidence." There are lots of "ahas" for both women and men.

Mandino, Og, *The Greatest Salesman in the World* 1968 and *The Greatest Salesman in the World, Part II – The End of the Story* 1988, New York: Bantam Books. Og's classic story of Hafid, the camel boy, has inspired millions throughout the world. The long-awaited sequel is just as powerful. It features "The Ten Vows of Success" which serve as a blueprint for ageless application.

Peck, M. Scott, M.D., *The Different Drum: Community Making and Peace*, New York: Touchstone (Simon & Schuster) 1987. Here, the author of *The Road Less Traveled* challenges us to take another journey in self-awareness: to achieve, through the creative experience of community, a new "connectedness" and wholeness.

Career Planning

Here are five books for your consideration in this important area – one that is the standard in the field, one from a well-known career development specialist, one brand new book that

I think will excite your interest, one directed primarily at recent college graduates, and one specifically for those who may be considering the possibility of becoming professional speakers.

Bolles, Richard Nelson, *What Color Is Your Parachute: A Practical Manual for Job-Hunters and Career-Changers*, Berkeley, CA: Ten Speed Press, New Edition Annually. The best-known and best-selling book in the field, this is a "must have" resource for anyone who is considering looking for a new job or changing careers. It is entertaining reading as well as loaded with ideas. In addition to the annual *Parachute* updates, two other books by Dick Bolles are also highly relevant to our subject here: *The Three Boxes of Life, And How To Get Out Of Them* and *Where Do I Go With The Rest Of My Life*, also published by Ten Speed Press.

Kaye, Dr. Beverly, *5 Crucial Career Questions: The Career Systems Approach to Career Development*, Washington, D.C.: Career Systems Inc. 1991. This primer on career development is a practical, up-to-date treatment of the process of self-assessment, goal setting and action planning. I have known and admired Bev Kaye's work for years. Author of *Up Is Not The Only Way*, she is one of the most respected organization consultants specializing in career development. She has done an outstanding job of pulling together a simple, yet powerful, approach to making career planning work.

Lowstuter, Clyde C. and David P. Robertson, *In Search of the Perfect Job: 12 Proven Steps to Get the Job You Really Want*, New York: McGraw-Hill 1992. I had the privilege of reviewing and making editorial suggestions on this brand new book by the principals of one of the fastest growing outplacement firms in the Midwest. In my judgment, it provides a major breakthrough for people in all walks of life who are interested in changing jobs or who may be facing one of the most traumatic experiences of their lives – the loss of a position to which they have devoted years of dedicated effort. This book is both practical and readable. The sections related to resume-writing and networking are the best I have seen in any book on the subject.

Powell, C. Randall, *Career Planning Today*, Dubuque, IA: Kendall/Hunt 1981. This is an interesting and entertaining book that takes you through three phases: Planning Your Career, *Organizing Your Career,* and *Controlling Your Career.* Written by the manager of the college placement program at Indiana University, it is especially useful for recent college graduates.

Walters, Dottie and Lillet Walters, *Speak and Grow Rich,* Englewood Cliffs, NJ: Prentice-Hall 1989. Professional speaking is an important part of my career. It is a business that many people who are experts consider at some point in their careers. This book, written by two pros who know that business, is the most complete one on the subject that I am aware of. It covers everything from how to get started to effective promotion to development and sale of speaker products. If you are thinking about professional speaking, you need this book.

Business Planning

The books identified here will focus on what you need to do in managing your business whether that be in private practice, as part of a professional services firm, or within a larger, more diversified business. The descriptions will help you determine which ones are particularly applicable to you.

Below, Patrick J., George L. Morrisey, Betty L. Acomb, *The Executive Guide to Strategic Planning,* San Francisco: Jossey-Bass 1987. This is where many of the strategic planning concepts included in *Creating Your Future* evolved, although they have been *adapted* extensively to fit the personal planning perspective. This book provides a sound, experience-based process for making strategic planning work in any organization.

Davidson, Jeffrey P., *Avoiding the Pitfalls of Starting Your Own Business,* New York: Walker 1988. As stated in the Introduction, this is not a "how to" book, its a "here's what" book. Jeff presents a sobering look at causes of entrepreneurial failure, related to such things as inadequate financing, lack of a business plan and unrealistic expectations, which are avoidable with proper planning.

Dible, Donald M., *Up Your Own Organization: A handbook for today's entrepreneur,* Reston, VA: Reston Publishing (Prentice-Hall) 1986. This no-nonsense entrepreneur's guide is written by a man who has been there many times. Don provides an inside out look at what is involved in true entrepreneurship, the various elements of a business plan and how to put them together, plus some practical approaches to gaining access to money sources. It is must reading for those in start-up ventures.

Edwards, Paul and Sarah, *Working From Home: Everything You Need to Know about Living and Working under the Same Roof*, Los Angeles: Tarcher 1985. This is a complete reference book for people working at home from two people who have made it work for them. Paul and Sarah are the perfect role models for a family-run small business. Of particular value is the section on computerizing your home office.

Entrepreneur Magazine, *Entrepreneur's Guide to Business Start-ups*, Irvine, CA: Entrepreneur Inc. 1990. Packaged in loose-leaf format, this is a manual that will lead you by the hand through the process of starting a business. It begins with helping you establish criteria for choosing the right business and takes you through all aspects such as market research, financing, sales and pricing, including practical guidance on when and how to sell your business or practice.

LeBoeuf, Michael, Ph.D., *The Greatest Management Principle in the World*, New York, Putnam 1985. Simply stated, the Greatest Management Principle is "The things that get rewarded get done." This is a solid, highly readable book that provides practical ideas, using this principle, for managing others, managing your boss, and managing yourself. Read it; you'll be glad you did.

Morrisey, George L., Patrick J. Below, Betty L. Acomb, *The Executive Guide to Operational Planning*, San Francisco: Jossey-Bass 1988. This is the sequel to *The Executive Guide to Strategic Planning* (identified above) which focuses on the short term or annual business planning process. It is a practical, straight forward guide to help any responsible manager develop and implement specific plans that will support the organization's strategic plan.

Odiorne, George S., *The Human Side of Management: Management by Integration and Self-Control*, Lexington, MA: Heath 1987. I could not complete this bibliography without at least one book from my colleague, mentor and friend to whose memory this book is dedicated. While most of his books focus primarily on management within organizations, this one, in particular, transcends that perspective. It provides a thoroughly up-to-date treatise on how to work with human resources, particularly recent college graduates, to ensure a mutually-fulfilling on-the-job experience.

Shenson, Howard L., *Shenson on Consulting: Success Strategies from the Consultant's Consultant*, New York: Wiley 1990. The late Howard Shenson helped thousands of consultants organize their practices in a sound, business-like manner. This book, one of many he has written, provides a well-rounded picture for building and maintaining a successful consulting practice.

Tregoe, Benjamin B. and John W. Zimmerman, *Top Management Strategy: What It Is and How to Make It Work*, New York: Simon & Schuster 1980. This clear, definitive work on the meaning and application of strategy is the one from which the concept of the "driving force" (covered in Chapter 3) was first derived. It is important reading for anyone wishing to have a clearer focus on the future direction of their business.

Financial Planning

If I had the money that I have spent over the years on books, newsletters, and self-teaching courses on financial planning (most of which I read either superficially or not at all), I would have enough to make a sizable addition to my investment portfolio. While I am still hoping to find that one resource that will make this aspect of personal planning clear as crystal and easy to work with, here are a few that seem to come close.

Blechman, Bruce and Jay Conrad Levinson, *Guerrilla Financing*, Boston: Houghton Mifflin 1991. Although I must confess that the word "Guerrilla" creates some unwelcome images in my mind, this book does provide excellent, understandable insights on getting financial backing for a small business. Particularly interesting is the chapter "101 Guerrilla Financing Techniques" for solving "financial problems that everyone else said *could not be solved.*"

Jones, H. Stanley, CPA, *Planning Your Financial Future*, New York: Wiley 1988. A major premise that Stan puts forth is that everyone needs a personal financial planner. Consequently, he provides guidance in the selection process so that you are more likely to establish a relationship with one who will serve your needs more effectively. The book also includes an understandable overview of the total financial planning process which is a lot more than just making the right investments. As such, it will help you ask the *right* questions when you are interviewing prospective financial planners.

Lerner, Joel, *Financial Planning for the Utterly Confused, Third Edition*, New York: McGraw-Hill 1991. While this book is light on financial *planning* as such, it provides a clear explanation of the various investment opportunities available. (Do you understand the difference between Ginnie Maes, Fannie Maes and Freddie Macs, for example?) It also clarifies the different types of personal retirement plans – IRA, 401(k), SEP, Keogh, etc. – so you can determine which plan, or combination, makes the most sense for you.

Lindsey, Jennifer, *Start-Up Money*, New York: Wiley 1989. This book is particularly targeted at small business owners who are seeking $100,000 in debt or equity capital – which would fit many professionals in private practice. While focused more on commodity businesses, most of the concepts and techniques covered here are equally applicable to a personal services business that needs a modest amount of capital to either get started or expand.

Home and Family

I am especially fond of the following two books which are highly supportive of our concept of a "balanced life."

Bramson, Robert M., Ph.D. and Susan Bramson, *The Stressless Home: A Practical Guide to Making Your Home a Haven of Comfort and Tranquility*, New York: Ballantine 1987. This is a delightful, practical book about developing caring relationships and building a mutually-supportive family plan that can make your home a place of joy. Bob's and Susan's concept of constructing a Planning Network as a means of addressing "The Gentle Art of Containing Chaos" is an especially useful personal planning tool.

Batten, Joe D., Wendy Havemann, Bill Pearce and Gail Pedersen, *Tough Minded Parenting*, Nashville, TN: Broadman Press 1991. Joe Batten, together with his two daughters and a close friend and colleague, has applied his "tough minded" (resilient) philosophy to one of the most important professions in the world today — that of being a parent. "Parenting is our most important single human activity, and children are our most important product" presents a frightening challenge for many. Yet it is an essential part of the balanced life I have been stressing. This book will help place that challenge in a positive perspective.

Writing/Publishing

Writing does not come easily for most people, even those, like me, who have been doing it for some time. Here are three books that will help you get started on the road to publishing.

Burgett, Gordon, *Self-Publishing to Tightly-Targeted Markets*, Santa Maria, CA: Communication Unlimited 1989. If you are considering writing a book related to your professional specialty which may have a solid, but limited, potential market, this is the book to get. Gordon's premise is straightforward: "If you know something that others will pay to know, they will pay to know it by many ways and by many means." It starts with marketing, moves on to writing, then to expanded marketing.

Mager, Robert F., *The How to Write a Book Book*, Belmont: CA: Lake Publishing Co. 1984. When Bob sent me an autographed first edition of this book, I immediately ordered 25 copies and sent them to colleagues who had been talking about getting published. Written in his inimitable humorous style, this book will lead you by the hand from conception through publication.

Poynter, Dan, *The Self-Publishing Manual, 5th Edition*, Santa Barbara, CA: Para Publishing 1989. Dan is considered by many, including me, to be the guru of self-publishing. He has the most complete inventory I know of available books and other resources on the ins and outs of self-publishing, many authored by others as well as himself. This book is a valuable "soup to nuts" guide for authors or would-be authors. Write to him at Para Publishing, P.O. Box 4232, Santa Barbara, CA 93140-4232 and ask to be put on his mailing list for his newsletter and catalog.

Blank
Worksheets

ON THE FOLLOWING PAGES are 18 different worksheets that have been introduced in this book. Permission is granted for reproduction of these worksheets for the individual use of the book owner. No other reproduction is permitted without the express written permission of the publisher.

YOUR CAREER PATH OPTIONS

CAREER PATH	N.A.	Am Now	Do Now	This Year	Next Year	Future
Full time student						
Part time student						
Professional employee						
Manager						
Executive						
Private practice						
Professional firm staff						
Professional firm manager						
Professional firm principal/partner						
Educator						
Other						
Career change						

STRATEGIC VALUES DECISION MATRIX

	1 Independence/Freedom	2 Financial Return	3 Financial Security	4 Challenge/Risk Taking	5 Family Considerations	6 Geographical Focus	7 Service to Others	8 Personal Legacy/Estate	9 Professional/Peer Recog.	10 Professional Relationships	11 Power/Influence	12 Principles/Ethics	13	14	TOTAL "X'S"
1 Independence/Freedom															
2 Financial Return															
3 Financial Security															
4 Challenge/Risk Taking															
5 Family Considerations															
6 Geographical Focus															
7 Service to Others															
8 Personal Legacy/Estate															
9 Professional/Peer Recog.															
10 Professional Relationships															
11 Power/Influence															
12 Principles/Ethics															
13															
14															

	1	2	3	4	5	6	7	8	9	10	11	12	13	14
VERTICAL (spaces)														
HORIZONTAL (X's)														
TOTAL														
RANK ORDER														

INSTRUCTIONS

1. Review list of strategic values and eliminate any that do not apply to your situation; add any additional ones that may be appropriate on the blank lines, repeating each under the corresponding number at the top.

2. Evaluate #1 against #2. If #1 is more important, place "X" in box under #2; if #1 is less important, leave blank. Repeat with each remaining number. (Work only within the triangle of white boxes.) Continue to next line; repeat.

3. Total "X's" across for each number; enter in HORIZONTAL box at bottom; total "spaces" down for each number; enter in VERTICAL box at bottom; add both HORIZONTAL and VERTICAL for TOTAL.

4. Largest number under TOTAL will be #1 in RANK ORDER; next largest will be #2, etc. If two or more alternatives have the same TOTAL, RANK ORDER is determined by comparing each subjectively against the others.

Copyright © 1974, 1989 by George L. Morrisey, The Morrisey Group, Buena Park, California.

DECISION MATRIX

TOTAL "X'S"

Column headers (top): 1 | 2 | 3 | 4 | 5 | 6 | 7 | 8 | 9 | 10 | 11 | 12 | 13 | 14

Row labels (left): 1, 2, 3, 4, 5, 6, 7, 8, 9, 10, 11, 12, 13, 14

	1	2	3	4	5	6	7	8	9	10	11	12	13	14
VERTICAL (spaces)														
HORIZONTAL (X's)														
TOTAL														
RANK ORDER														

INSTRUCTIONS

1. List each item twice – once on horizontal line, again on corresponding vertical line.

2. Evaluate #1 against #2. If more important, place "X" in box under #2; if less important, leave blank. Repeat with each remaining number. (Work only within the triangle of white boxes.) Continue to next line; repeat.

3. Total "X's" across for each number; enter in HORIZONTAL box at bottom; total "spaces" down for each number; enter in VERTICAL box at bottom; add both HORIZONTAL and VERTICAL for TOTAL.

4. Largest number under TOTAL will be #1 in RANK ORDER; next largest will be #2, etc. If two or more alternatives have the same TOTAL, RANK ORDER is determined by comparing each subjectively against the others. (This will not happen unless there is an inconsistency in your analysis.)

Copyright © 1974, 1989 by George L. Morrisey, The Morrisey Group, Buena Park, California

CHANGING YOUR STRATEGIC DIRECTION

1. What is my current driving force? Why has this been important?

2. What should be my future driving force? Why is that important?

3. What other major values need to be taken into consideration?

4. What changes need to be addressed to meet the requirements of my future driving force?

CLARIFYING YOUR PERSONAL AND PROFESSIONAL MISSION

1a. What business and/or profession *am* I in personally?

1b. What business and/or profession *would I like* to be in? (What do I really enjoy?)

1c. What business and/or profession *should* I be in?

2. What is my basic purpose in business and in life?

3. What are or should be my principal business functions and roles, present and future?

4. What is unique or distinctive about what I can bring to my business/profession?

5. Who are or should be my principal customers, clients, or users?

6. What are the principal market segments, present and future, in which I am most effective?

7. What is different about my personal business position from what it was three to five years ago?

8. What is likely to be different about my personal business position three to five years in the future?

---

9. What are my principal economic concerns?

10. What are or should be my principal sources of income?

11. What philosophical issues, personal values and priorities are important to my future?

13. What special considerations do I have in regard to the following (as applicable)?

- Board of directors or other outside group

- Employer(s)

- Partners or associates

- Staff

- Customers, clients, or users

- Vendors or suppliers

- Professional colleagues

- Professional associations

- Family

- Church or community

- Myself

- Other (specify)

SELECTING YOUR AREAS OF STRATEGIC CONCERN

Potential Areas	Category			Priority	Selection	Notes
	A	B	C	1, 2, etc.		
Personal						
Family/personal rel.						
Health, rest & recreation						
Cultural pursuits						
Service to others						
Retirement						
Career Growth						
Education						
Cert./lic./prof. desig.						
Research/study						
Publications						
Affiliations						
Work experience						
Business Development						
Services/products						
Clients/customers/mkts.						
Marketing/sales						
Associates/staffing						
Business operations						
Financial						
Cash flow						
Capital requirements						
Pricing, gross/net profit						
Net worth						

CRITICAL ISSUE ANALYSIS OF PERSONAL AREAS

Critical Issue

Supporting Data

Root Causes (if needed)

Conclusions and/or Alternative Courses of Action

CRITICAL ISSUE ANALYSIS OF CAREER GROWTH AREAS

Critical Issue

Supporting Data

Root Causes (if needed)

Conclusions and/or Alternative Courses of Action

CRITICAL ISSUE ANALYSIS OF BUSINESS DEVELOPMENT AREAS

Critical Issue

Supporting Data

Root Causes (if needed)

Conclusions and/or Alternative Courses of Action

CRITICAL ISSUE ANALYSIS OF FINANCIAL AREAS

Critical Issue

Supporting Data

Root Causes (if needed)

Conclusions and/or Alternative Courses of Action

CURRENT SERVICE/PRODUCT ASSESSMENT

SERVICES/PRODUCTS	CAPABILITY	DEMAND	COMPETITION	FEE/PRICE	COST	DESIRE

FUTURE SERVICE/PRODUCT ASSESSMENT

SERVICES/PRODUCTS	CAPABILITY	DEMAND	COMPETITION	FEE/PRICE	COST	DESIRE	PREPARATION	TIMING

CHECKLIST FOR DETERMINING
YOUR PREFERRED INDIVIDUAL CLIENT/CUSTOMER PROFILE

AGE RANGE: ____Infants/preschool ____ Preteens ____Teens
____20-35 ____36-50 ____50-65 ____ Retirees ____ Aged
Comments:

GENDER/MARITAL STATUS: ____Female ____Male____Either
____Couples ____ Married ____Single ____Divorced/Separated
____Widowed
Comments:

OCCUPATIONS: ___Business Owners____Professionals____Managers
____Executives ____ Sales____Technical____Blue Collar____Students
____Unemployed
____Others (Specify) _____

Comments:

ANNUAL INCOME: ____$0-10,000 ____$10,000-25,000____$25,0000-
50,000____$50,000-100,000___$100,000-500,000___$500,000+

Comments:

GEOGRAPHICAL AREA:___Local___Commuting Distance___In-State
____In-Region ____National ____North America ____Worldwide
____Other (Specify)_____
Comments:

METHOD OF PAYMENT:___Cash___Credit Card___Open Account
____Installment___Retainer___Company Charge ___Insurance
____Other (Specify) _____

Comments:

OTHER CONSIDERATIONS:

Use these factors as a springboard, adding any others that are particularly relevant to you and the type of practice you have. Under each factor, first place a check mark (√) alongside those you are willing and able to serve; then go back and place an asterisk (*) alongside those that constitute your preferred clientele. (This is designed for internal use and will not, necessarily, be shown to clients.)

CHECKLIST FOR DETERMININGYOUR PREFERRED ORGANIZATIONAL CLIENT/CUSTOMER PROFILE

TYPE OF BUSINESS:___Manufacturer___Retail___Wholesale
___Distributor___Service___Government___Not-for-Profit
___Other (Specify)_____

Comments:

SIZE (NUMBER OF EMPLOYEES):___1-10___11-50___51-100___101-500
___501-1,000___1,000-5,000)___5,000-10,000___10,000+

Comments:

TYPE OF ORGANIZATION:___Proprietorship___Partnership
___Corporation___Family Owned___Single Location___Multiple Locations
____Other (Specify) _____

Comments:

GEOGRAPHICAL CONSIDERATIONS:___Local___Commuting Distance
___In-State___In-Region___National___North America___Worldwide
____Other (Specify) _____

Comments:

SPECIAL CHARACTERISTICS:___Fast Growth___High Tech___Low Tech
___Centralized___Decentralized___Franchise___Turnaround
____Other (Specify) _____

Comments:

DECISION MAKERS/INFLUENCERS : (Mark *M* if principal Decision
Maker; *I* if Decision Influencer):___CEO/COO___Finance/Administration
___Human Resources ____Production ____Purchasing ____Sales ____Other
(Specify) _____

Comments:

Use these factors as a springboard, adding any others that are particularly relevant to you and the type of practice you have. Under each factor, first place a check mark (√) alongside those you are willing and able to serve; then go back and place an asterisk (*) alongside those that constitute your preferred clientele. (This is designed for internal use and will not, necessarily, be shown to clients.)

LONG TERM OBJECTIVES FORMULATION

Selection Process

1. Identify strategic areas that need to be considered for potential long term objectives. Determine which are the six to eight most important.

2. Identify, within each area, the potential results that will move you closer to the fulfillment of your mission. These results should be broad in scope and highly visible.

3. Select and reach consensus, with others who are affected, on no more than six to eight long term objectives that will enable you to be positioned where you want to be at some point in the future. Where possible, write them in an objectives format: "To have (or become) [the result] by [year]."

Strategic Areas   *Long Term Objectives*

Criteria for Validating a Long-Term Objective

1. **Is it measurable or verifiable?** Will you, and others affected, be able to recognize it when it happens?

2. **Is it achievable or feasible?** What major efforts or significant changes must take place in order to achieve the objective? What is the likelihood of these happening?

3. **Is it flexible or adaptable?** Will it take into account changing circumstances and new opportunities?

4. **Is it consistent with the rest of the plan?** Does this objective move you closer to the positions that have been taken as you constructed your mission statement and completed your strategic analysis?

ALTERNATIVE EVALUATION CHART

OBJECTIVE:

ALTERNATIVES	Impact	Cost	Can I	Will I	Other	Notes

First, brainstorm alternatives, then eliminate those that are impractical.
Next, evaluate the remaining alternatives vertically against each of the criteria.
Alternative evaluation methods: High-Medium-Low; rank order; scale of 1-5; assigned weights related to importance of criteria; add up total "score" for each.
Copyright © 1974, 1989 by George L. Morrisey

STRATEGIC ACTION PLAN FORMAT

Long Term Objective:

What	When	How Much	Who	On Track?

PLANNING CHECKLIST

	N.A.	O.K.	Do Now	This Year	Next Year	Future
PLANNING PROCESS						
Career path choices						
Strategic values						
Personal & professional mission						
Organizational mission						
Strategic analysis						
Personal						
Professional growth						
Business development						
Financial						
Long term objectives						
Strategic action plans						
Other						
OTHER PEOPLE						
Spouse/life partner						
Children						
Other family						
Employer						
Professional colleagues						
Friends						
Facilitator						
Other						
IMPLEMENTATION						
Strategic planning notebook						
Review schedule						
Graphic display/charts						
Plan modification						
Other						

Index